The Victorian *Fol Sage*

The Victorian *Fol Sage*

Comparative Readings
on Carlyle, Emerson, Melville, and Conrad

Camille R. La Bossière

Lewisburg
Bucknell University Press
London and Toronto: Associated University Presses

© 1989 by Associated University Presses, Inc.

All rights reserved. Authorization to photocopy items for internal or personal use, or the internal or personal use of specific clients, is granted by the copyright owner, provided that a base fee of $10.00, plus eight cents per page, per copy is paid directly to the Copyright Clearance Center, 27 Congress Street, Salem, Massachusetts 01970. [0-8387-5145-8/88 $10.00 + 8¢ pp, pc.]

Associated University Presses
440 Forsgate Drive
Cranbury, NJ 08512

Associated University Presses
25 Sicilian Avenue
London WC1A 2QH, England

Associated University Presses
P.O. Box 488, Port Credit
Mississauga, Ontario
Canada L5G 4M2

The paper used in this publication meets the requirements of the American National Standard for Permanence of Paper for Printed Library Materials Z39.48-1984.

Library of Congress Cataloging-in-Publication Data

La Bossière, Camille R.
  The Victorian Fol sage.

  Bibliography: p.
  Includes index.
  1. English prose literature—19th century—History and criticism.   2. American prose literature—19th century—History and criticism.   I. Title.
PR781.L3   1989   828'.808'09   87-48005
ISBN 0-8387-5145-8 (alk. paper)

PRINTED IN THE UNITED STATES OF AMERICA

*à mon père,
à ma mère,
Camille Augustin,
Hermine Joséphine*

Contents

Preface   9

Introduction: The Victorian *Fol Sage*   15
1 Carlyle and Montaigne: Their Silent Conversation   20
2 Emerson's Divine Comedy   38
3 Melville's Mute Glass   59
4 Of Blindness in Conrad's Spectacular Universe   86
Postscript: The Consolation of Folly   98

Notes   102
Select Bibliography   120
Index   129

Preface

THIS book's comparative reading of four rhetorical responses to the principle of the *coincidentia oppositorum* aims to contribute to the history of wisdom's decline as the principle of knowledge and certainty in the nineteenth century. Comparison of the Victorian sage's "musical thought" and the skepticism of Montaigne, with its studied unscience and endless self-contradiction, serves to advance the argument that the disparagement of logical analysis and ethics in favor of imaginative synthesis and poetics could hardly have helped but make the work of the public teacher of wisdom nugatory. As Eugen Biser remarks, the falling off of wisdom as "insight into the order of nature and history so well-developed that it can be the rule of life" can be traced to the failure of modern thought to establish and comprehend "the opposition between abstract and concrete, universal and particular, idea and reality."[1] A harlequin artist and rhetorician of the coincidence of opposites, the Victorian sage contributed substantially to that failure. And there are elements in his modern reception to corroborate such an estimate. The current tendency among the students of the Victorian purveyor of wisdom to place little if any value on his dogma does more than simply register a change in critical fashion or moral belief. Their appraisal faithfully translates the contradiction built into and undermining his enterprise. Carlyle, for example, who aspired to the role of prophet to his age, is at his best not as a provider of life-guidance, by A. L. Le Quesne's reckoning in 1982, but as an artist *malgré lui*, a seer with "double vision," and a player adept at keeping opposites "in balance."[2]

The choice of the first two authors for study, Carlyle and Emerson, was virtually dictated by history. As James Joyce recalled in 1900, they were (with Rousseau) "those giants" who before Ibsen had held "empire over the thinking world in modern times."[3] Carlyle and Emerson dominate in an age remarkable for the number and variety of its moral guides and teachers. Melville, the subject of the third chapter, was chosen for the reason that his entire work turns on the skepticism fundamental to the wisdom of Carlyle and Emerson, which he takes to its logical conclusion, of self-betrayal or self-consumption: "WISDOM IS VAIN," Melville's poem "The Conflict of Convictions" pronounces. Their contradiction of each other and themselves demonstrates the folly of would-be sages. The selection of Conrad, finally, was made at the perceptive suggestion of John Holloway's classic study, *The Victorian Sage: Studies in Argument* (1953), where the modern writer of ambiguous fabulations implicitly figures as the *terminus ad quem* of the Victorian teacher of wisdom. Not a knowing seer in a democracy of the blind, the Conradian artist renders the truth of himself and humanity as the intimate alliance of contradictions, and consequently renounces the vocation of sage. For Conrad the artist as for Montaigne the skeptic, "l'individu se modèle selon un devenir étranger à toute fin éthique."[4]

It goes without saying that the writer of this book has sympathy with the authors he considers. The humility of *que sais-je?* is attractive, of course, chastening as it is to rationalism of the overweening kind. There is much to endear in professions of unknowing and much to divert in the play of self-contradiction. He must, on the other hand and by the same token, demur at the earnest imperialism latent in the self-consuming (but hardly self-effacing) artificer's way of reading the world: it is "antidiscursive and antirational; rather than distinguishing, it resolves, and in the world it delivers the lines of demarcation between places and things fade in the light of an all-embracing unity."[5] Like darkness in its erasing of differences, the light of unreason tends to be omnivorous. In the absence of reason, everything goes. Nor is this writer persuaded of the pedagogical value of that drowsiness which unreason, again like darkness, has a tendency to induce. As Walter Kaufmann reminds us, the illumination provided by antirational and antidiscursive works can be soporific: it "often puts the critical sense to sleep."[6] "The Consolation of Folly," the postscript to this study engaging Carlyle, Emerson, Melville, and Conrad, the nature and method of which are designed to respect those differences that make similitude and therefore genuine dialogue possible, draws out that point. Since it is fundamentally negative, the value of unreason as an instrument for teaching (or criticism) is somewhat doubtful and, to the student prizing discursive or rational understanding, necessarily short-lived.

And if life is a dream, as skeptics and synthetic night-thinkers are inclined to say with Montaigne, this writer is persuaded that it is not his alone. There is, for example, the matter of those gifts from others that went into the making of *The Victorian "Fol Sage"* and that he is delighted to record. My thanks to Gerald Morgan, Emeritus Professor of literature and philosophy at the Royal Roads Military College of Canada, for his guidance in the literature of wisdom and Conradiana; to John Spencer Hill and David Lyle Jeffrey, of the University of Ottawa, for their valuable questions, corrections, counsel, and encouragement; to George Thomson, Dominic Manganiello, Irene Makaryk, and Ina Ferris, also of the University of Ottawa, for putting useful suggestions in my path; to Murray Baumgarten, of the University of California (Santa Cruz), Bill Bonney, of Mississippi State University, and Leo Damrosch, Jr., of the University of Maryland, for the present of books and ideas; to E. D. Blodgett, of the University of Alberta, and J. J. Healy, of Carleton University, for their kind support of this project at its inception; to Mrs. Oukje De Bruyn, of Ottawa, for her translation of Jacob Revius; to the School of Graduate Studies at the University of Ottawa, for timely research grants; and to the Social Sciences and Humanities Research Council of Canada, for the leave fellowship that made the writing of this book possible. And not least, there is the growing debt of gratitude to my wife and son, Diane and Paul.

"Logical thinking is . . . of indispensable use in giving clearness and compactness to our knowledge, and enabling us, with light mastery, to impart it to others." The words are John Sterling's.[7] My hope is that the reader who finds them congenial will come away from *The Victorian "Fol Sage"* as a whole with some measure of satisfaction.

The first chapter of this book was developed from an article, "Of Silence, Doubt, and Imagination: Carlyle's Conversation with Montaigne," which appeared in *English Studies in Canada* 10 (1984): 62–76.

The Victorian *Fol Sage*

Introduction: The Victorian *Fol Sage*

Let us go down into the blind world.
—Dante, *Inferno*

The wise contradict themselves.
—Wilde, "Phrases and Philosophies for the Use of the Young"

"THE Plato of Walter Pater is Montaigne's Plato," Harold Bloom recalls in *Figures of Capable Imagination* (1976).[1] The student of Socrates is the skeptical dialectician engaged in the subversion of all philosophies, taking himself for subject and object and public: "Just there, lies the validity of the method—in a dialogue, an endless dialogue, with one's self," in the words Bloom cites from Pater's *Plato and Platonism* (1893).[2] For Walter E. Houghton, in *The Victorian Frame of Mind, 1830–1870* (1956), Pater's revival of "the scepticism of Hume" in the 1868 "Conclusion" to *The Renaissance* marks the waning of an age of faith in social, moral, and intellectual progress, which creed is pronounced moribund by the time of *Plato and Platonism* and Pater's discovery of "the beginning of the modern, relative spirit in Montaigne."[3] "*Que scais-je?* it [the age] cries."[4] "The father of Anglo-American Aestheticism," as Bloom's history repeats, "yielded up the great societal and religious hopes of the major Victorian prose-prophets, and urged us to abide in the mortal truths of perception and sensation."[5] Pater's position as skeptic and aesthete opposes him to Carlyle, for example, the principal of the "teachers" with "moral preoccupations" featured in John Holloway's *The Victorian Sage: Studies in Argument* (1953).[6] As Holloway affirms in his conclusion, which includes a defense of the sage's way of seeing and teaching, the chief thing the Victorian purveyors of wisdom have in common is the poetical articulation of moral principles based on "what they think the world is like."[7] Their advocacy of convictions of practical concern in human life gives a measure of the distance separating them from Pater and the long line of skeptics who, like Hume in *A Treatise of Human Nature,* have reckoned the attempt to infer *ought* and *ought not* from *is* and *is not* an absurd and comical enterprise.[8]

Strong as the disjunction is, in principle, between the skeptical Pater and the Victorian teacher of practical wisdom, there is considerable history and practice to sustain a reading of their relationship that sees them not quite so far apart. In 1848, for example, more than two decades before Pater's *The Renaissance* and some ten years after John Sterling's widely influential article linking Montaigne with Socrates and the Shakespeare of *Hamlet*,[9] Charles-Augustin Sainte-Beuve imagined Saint-Évremond, Hume, himself, and perhaps all of his contemporaries as a line of followers in Montaigne's funeral cortege.[10] Charles Dédéyan's more recent history, *Montaigne chez ses amis anglo-saxons* (1943), concurs, beginning as it does in the seventeenth century its continuous tracking of the *Essais* through English romanticism to the time of *Plato and Platonism*.[11] And additional confirmation of Sainte-Beuve's picture of 1848 appears in Holloway's portrait of the Victorian sage. "It is not altogether clear how these . . . are legitimate in any way at all," Holloway's introduction declares, questioning the authority of the sage's teachings. The question does not go unanswered. "It becomes clear," *The Victorian Sage* subsequently concludes, "that . . . his message finds part of its sanction, maybe the only solid part, in what we actually see or feel: in our environment or our emotions."[12] Clearly, Holloway's study has led him to the place of the Montaigne-like Pater, who "urged us to abide in the mortal truths of perception and sensation."[13] The conclusion is understandable: the sage's "disparagement of logic" in favor of "the essentially individualist methods of the artist"[14] draws the mind steadily to that end. Though it does not say so explicitly, Holloway's study hints at a contradiction of end and means making of the sage's vocation a calling to suicide.

Indirect suggestion of the subversive nature of Holloway's work and the wisdom of the age he examines comes early in *The Victorian Sage,* with two references to Conrad. Wisdom, in the view of the model teacher Carlyle, is "somehow an opening of the eyes," and the sage a seer gifted with "insight that is abnormally keen."[15] That notion invites comparison with Conrad's account of his own purpose in the 1897 Preface to *The Nigger of the "Narcissus"*: "before all, to make you *see*. That, and no more, and it is everything. If I succeed, you shall find there according to your deserts: encouragement, consolation, fear, charm—all you demand—and, perhaps, also that glimpse of truth for which you have forgotten to ask."[16] And the method by which Carlyle strives to make his reader see is that of the artist. He rejects direct rational argument in favor of oblique rhetorical suggestion. The sage makes his appeal "to imagination rather than logic" in his effort, by the power of figurative and musical language to move the emotions, to convince his public of the truth of his insights.[17] Again, Conrad provides the analogue: "He who wants to persuade should put his trust not in the right argument, but in the right word," Holloway cites from "A Familiar Preface" to *A Personal Record*.[18] The comparison is instructive and has a certain historical justness, for Conrad did respond to Carlyle on a number of occasions, particularly in the first decade of his career as artist. The final paragraph of *The Nigger of the "Narcissus,"* for example, imitates the rhetoric of the last sentence of *Sartor Resartus*, a work mentioned by title near the beginning of *Youth*.[19] There is substance as well in the Carlyle-Conrad correspondence: both rejected the traditional formal logic as the way to underlying truth.[20] "To *know;* to get into the truth of anything, is ever a mystic act,—of which the best Logics can but babble on the surface," cited by Holloway from *On Heroes and Hero Worship*,[21] expresses a fundamental Conradian conviction, and appears on the same page as Carlyle's translation of the Novalis dictum that provides the epigraph of *Lord Jim:* "It is certain . . . my Conviction gains infinitely, the moment another soul will believe in it."[22] Holloway makes a telling point, that Carlyle the sage and Conrad the artist share common ground.

What Holloway does not mention, however, is that "A Familiar Preface" to *A Personal Record* shows Conrad's dissociation of the artist from the teacher of wisdom at its most overt. Conrad insists in that preface that he is never to be mistaken for "a sage" or "a moralist" concerned with teaching others how they should live. The business of the artist is to render justice to the truth of the world as it is—which is to say, as he sees it reflected in himself. That, and no more. As the Preface to *The Nigger of the "Narcissus"* affirms, "the artist appeals to that part of our being which is not dependent on wisdom." He does not "appeal to those qualities of our being that fit us best for the hazardous enterprise of living." In view of that abiding conviction in Conrad, his choice of Carlyle's "The Hero as Prophet" as the source for *Lord Jim*'s epigraph involves an irony expressive of his dissent from the vocation of the Victorian sage. Damning the "spiritual paralysis" that comes of the skeptic's "spiritual legerdemain," Carlyle's lecture advocates "the way of preaching and conviction" represented by Mahomet, and offers as a test of the prophet's authority and trustworthiness that his words have provided "life guidance" to millions of people for more than twelve hundred years.[23] It would be difficult to conceive of an advocacy and an intention more alien to the work of Conrad, who reserves a special scorn for gospel preachers claiming such special insight or righteousness as to justify their assumption of moral authority over others.

The Conradian artist's convictions are not those of the teacher of morals confident in the certainty of his revelation. They are but the convictions of the truth of his sense impressions or ambiguous feelings. As Eloise Knapp Hay illustrates in "Impressionism Limited" (1976), Conrad is more of a mind with the skeptic and aesthete than with the sage. Considering the combined force of Hume and Pater in Conrad's theory and practice of art, she aptly suggests that Hume's great question, " 'How do I move from the hard facts of sense data to certain knowledge?' . . . would make a good second epigraph for *Lord Jim*."[24] It goes without saying that neither the philosopher's perplexed dubitative nor Conrad's opaque fictive speculation gives a positive answer. Unlike Jim's father, a parson possessed of "certain knowledge of the Unknowable,"[25] the artist of sensation's truth can claim none of the knowledge necessary to qualify him for the responsible carrying out of the teacher's duties. The artist, like the skeptic, does not have the tools for the job. The man of doubt and imagination tutoring others in wisdom is engaged in a work as futile as that of the young aristocrat with a forked beard in *Heart of Darkness*: he has the job of making bricks without materials.[26] "L'artizan et sa besoigne se contrarient," Montaigne had written, anticipating the doleful Conradian joke: the man who erects works of wisdom and science with folly and ignorance is like a man building a stone wall without stones.[27] By indirection, Holloway's portrait of the Victorian sage places him in the company of such a fool. His composite picture of the public teacher of wisdom using the individualist methods of the artist, in fact, corresponds to the description of the skeptic in Richard William Church's *The Essays of Montaigne* (1857): he has "the depth of the seeing eye and the hearing ear . . . as poets and artists have it." The arch-individualist Montaigne, though, is no teacher of ethics, but a painter who, in accordance with the private nature of his art and his profession of invincible ignorance, declines to be "the representative of the wisdom of the public, or of any one's but his own."[28] An artist and a practitioner of folly, Montaigne disqualifies himself for the work of trustworthy sage: "une privée fantasie . . . n'a qu'une jurisdiction privée."[29] That is Conrad's conviction as well.

The four essays that follow, detecting Carlyle, Emerson, Melville, and Conrad in conversation with Montaigne and each other, turn on the fundamental contradiction between wisdom and art that impels the writing of the *Essais* and generates the skeptic's antic speculations. Since Socrates averred that "le principal office de la sagesse estoit distinguer les biens et les maux," as Montaigne facetiously recalls in "De l'yvrognerie," "nous autres, à qui le meilleur est toujours en vice, devons dire de mesme de la science de distinguer les vices; sans laquelle bien exacte le vertueux et le meschant demeurent meslez et incognus."[30] The joke is that Socrates himself, the wisest of men, does not fulfill the principal office of the sage, of distinguishing virtue from vice, what *ought* from what *ought not* to be done. His claim to wisdom is that he has none: what he knows is that he knows nothing. In the eyes of Montaigne, the confusing or blurring of ethical distinctions produced by the manifest contradictions in the sage's thought argues that Socrates, like Plato and Protagoras, does not mean to be taken seriously. Like the author of the *Essais,* a writing out of the endless interrogation of a chameleon self by a chameleon self about a chameleon self, he is but a poet and an entertainer, thinking and speaking, not for the public good, but solely for and about himself, for the sheer pleasure of the exercise. What coherence his utterances have is aesthetic only. As Montaigne's analogy in "De l'expérience" suggests, Plato's dialogues and symposia are the works of a musician. They are songs composed, "comme l'harmonie du monde, de choses contraires." The artist's enterprise, the composing of a *discordia concors* in tune with the syntax of unreason ruling the world, denies him the office of ethical guide: "Il faut qu'il s'en sçache servir en commun et les mesler . . . les biens et les maux, qui sont consubstantiels à nostre vie."[31] A wisdom based on what the world is like and taught by the individualist methods of the artist has built into it a contradiction announcing the sage's suicide and the triumph of unreason, folly, obscurity, and art. The Victorian sage prepares the way for Pater, his Montaigne, and his Montaigne's Plato.

1
Carlyle and Montaigne: Their Silent Conversation

> La fièvre continuelle . . . qui n'a point de remède.
> —Montaigne, "Divers evesnemens de mesme conseil"
>
> I sweated and shivered . . . hot and cold all over.
> —Conrad, *Heart of Darkness*

IN a letter of 17 October 1838, Emerson asked Carlyle for the name of the author whose article on Montaigne had recently appeared in the *London and Westminster Review*.[1] The answer, John Sterling, came in a letter of 7 November.[2] But Carlyle abstained from any discussion, as he always did when Montaigne entered their conversation. This silence, as with the others that punctuated the exchange of words between Emerson and Carlyle over nearly a half-century, has been interpreted as a sign of the differences separating them. According to Kenneth Marc Harris's *Carlyle and Emerson: Their Long Debate* (1978), Carlyle would "withdraw into silence, and take up something more promising" whenever "contradictions would arise that he could not resolve and would not accept."[3] Their disagreements, evidently, were substantial. "The temperament of the one was absolutely opposed to the temperament of the other," Henry James, Jr. observed in 1883;[4] and subsequent commentators have pretty much agreed with him. Ralph L. Rusk's *Life of Ralph Waldo Emerson* (1949), for example, states that "they were, in thought and character, plainly separated by a gap that could never be bridged,"[5] an estimate repeated in Joseph Slater's introduction to the 1964 edition of *The Correspondence of Emerson and Carlyle:* "in principle as in temperament, they stand poles apart," as opposite as "high and low, hot and cold, dark and light."[6] Their antagonism—"a contest of incompatible temperaments" for A. Abbott Ikeler in 1972[7]—rests, so

Harris's overview of that contest concludes, on the fundamental difference in their response to contradiction and illusion: Carlyle could not tolerate their presence, whereas Emerson could actually rejoice in it. "Long live true friends and Emersons,—and . . . 'May ne'er waur be amang us!'" Carlyle wrote in a letter of 25 September 1838, the reply to which included Emerson's inquiry after the author of "Montaigne and His Writings."[8] But conflict there was and would be, in a correspondence and an exchange of views increasingly marked by "long and ominous silences."[9]

Charles Dédéyan's *Montaigne chez ses amis anglo-saxons* (1943), an encyclopedic history of the presence of the *Essais* "dans le romantisme anglais et ses prolongements victoriens," similarly translates Carlyle's silence as a testament of opposition, though in this case in his relationship with Montaigne. The thought of the balancing skeptic, "une pensée individuelle et individualiste," and that of the volcanic dogmatist, "aux tendances collectives et sociales," represent "deux pôles, deux extrémités irréconciliables."[10] Understandably, in view of Dédéyan's identification of Emerson's voice with Montaigne's, the Montaigne-Carlyle relationship so read virtually duplicates the antipathy conventionally registered in comparisons of the two Anglo-Saxon writers. So basic are the differences that "toute alliance entre le penseur romantique et le philosophe humaniste nous paraît impossible," which complete divorce Carlyle himself is said to have realized.[11] Faced with that irreconcilability, the romantic thinker, in characteristic fashion, desisted from any conversation with his counterpart. The absence of the 1820 article on Montaigne from the editions of Carlyle's *Critical and Miscellaneous Essays* published in his lifetime provides additional testimony for Dédéyan's case. Only in 1899 is the neglected article from Brewster's *Edinburgh Encyclopaedia* given a place in a Carlyle miscellany.

But Emerson and Carlyle did speak with each other, of course. The Chelsea visionary who introduced Emerson's *Essays* (1841, 1844) into England, and the author of these, his literary agent in America, had much in common, as they both knew. Reflecting on his response to *Representative Men* in a letter of 19 July 1850, for example, Carlyle emphasized that their philosophies came together below the surface: ". . . tho' I see well enough what a great deep cleft divides us, in our ways of practically looking at this world,—I see also (as probably you do yourself) where the rock-strata, miles deep, unite again; and the two poor souls are at one. Poor devils!" His response to Emerson's portraits of Plato, Swedenborg, Montaigne, Shakespeare, Napoleon, and Goethe was "not without instructive interest" to Carlyle: he "generally dissented a little about the *end* of all these Essays," but only after "he had so lustily shouted 'Hear, hear!' all the way from the beginning up to that stage."[12] Though the ends to which their speculations took them were as distantly removed from each other as lighthearted optimism from muscular gloom, according to Rusk's account of Carlyle's dissent from *Representative Men*,[13] they shared elemental similarities. And the similarities were as wide as they were deep. Both writers rejected the "common school Logic" as an instrument of unbelief in an age of fervent materialism, seeing but darkness in the light shed by "the Torch of Science" and "the hand-lamp of . . . Attorney-Logic."[14] In search of a principle of illumination able to penetrate surfaces and so reveal underlying unitary truth, they withdrew from the utilitarian's "Logic-mill," as Carlyle termed the house of positive reason, to discover their master concepts in the same source, German Transcendentalism. Emerson, in fact, read German philosophy largely through the eyes of Coleridge and Carlyle. Like the author of *Sartor Resartus,* Emerson hoped to dream with his eyes open.[15]

If Carlyle's 1850 letter of response to *Representative Men* makes plain his awareness of a radical agreement with Emerson, it also tacitly suggests an analogous kinship with Montaigne. Having commented on "Plato; or, The Philosopher" and "Swedenborg; or, The Mystic," Carlyle stops short of the third essay, "Montaigne; or, The Sceptic," to confess to Emerson that their philosophies differ only as to outcomes. Again, Carlyle withdraws into silence before Montaigne, as though to confirm the representative skeptic's observation in the "Apologie de Raimond Sebond," that mental companions traveling along the same way often come to opposite ends: *par mesme voye une croyance contraire.*"[16] While divided, in Dédéyan's view, by a line of separation as wide as between freewheeling private exploration and earnest public service, Montaigne and Carlyle had much to say to each other in the transtemporal dialogue which is the history of ideas. They, too, shared common ground in the discarding of traditional or common-school logic as the way to underlying truth, and both raised enigma or unscience to a metaphysical principle. An exploration, historical and analytical, of the rock-strata at the center of Carlyle and Montaigne suggests the harmony as well as the dissonance between their voices, and thereby offers another account of Carlyle's tight-lipped response to Emerson's query. Silence, Carlyle tells us, is one expression of the "unspeakable" truth of the ironic and enigmatic dream-existence, otherwise available to man only by the synthetic logic of the imagination and its language, of symbol. While silence signifies the presence of irreconcilable differences, it also serves, in the Carlylean scheme of things, to express that underlying unity of opposite or disparate elements that is beyond the reach of reason.

"Montaigne est un grand ennemi de la logique scolastique," Sainte-Beuve records in the third volume of *Port-Royal* (1848).[17] The praise of science launching the famous "Apologie de Raimond Sebond," coupled with Montaigne's repeated attacks against Luther, whose *Disputatio contra scholasticam theologiam* (1517) had pronounced that "the whole of Aristotle is to theology as darkness is to light,"[18] would seem to give the lie to Sainte-Beuve's affirmation. "C'est, à la vérité, une très-utile et grande partie que la science. Ceux qui la mesprisent, tesmoignent assez leur bestise . . . ," Montaigne opens the Apology, and goes on to range the physician Sebond's *Theologia naturalis sive liber creaturarum* (1569)—"quelque quinte essence tirée de S. Thomas d'Aquin," he says he has been told—against the reformer (2.12.105–7). Here as elsewhere in the *Essais*, Montaigne diagnoses Lutheran self-reliance in interpretation as "une maladie." Since it is inherently divisive, multiplying contradictions and conflicts of opinion, the private judgment that denies any authority to external constraints, whether of reason or tradition, places all articles of faith "en doubte et à la balance": such a privileging of unreason and subjectivity unleashes "des guerres intestines" (2.12.105–6; 2.15.280). Setting out in the Apology to counter "les nouvelletez de Luther" (2.12.106)—or so it would seem—Montaigne presumably does not number himself among those whose scorning of science is sufficient testimony to their folly.

But Montaigne's attack against the folly of unreason is suicidal, in fact, and the title of his "Apologie de Raimond Sebond," ironic. As the self-conscious essayist takes pains with his work to show, it participates in the macabre comedy staged by the ostensibly learned and the wise as they contradict each other and themselves. The suicides lavishly deployed throughout the *Essais*—of men strangling, eating, starving, and stabbing themselves, for example, tearing out their own entrails, blowing themselves up or suffocating in an impenetrable privacy, in the coils of contradictory interpretations spun out of their own bowels—picture the very syntax of Montaigne's own activity: "l'un jugement en subvertissant l'autre sans cesse" (2.12.222). So wanting in logical coherence are his own essays, that he imagines them as bits of cloth to be stitched together in a thousand different and fantastical ways by a thousand different interpreters, or as inarticulated bodies, "rappiecez de divers membres, sans certaine figure" (2.12.203, 1.28.231). And when Montaigne finds irrational and risible the notion of an architect subverting his own design (2.12.187), he is himself the target of his wit, ranging himself in the company of builders trapped in an "infinity box," dismantling what he erects, "all in one process."[19] "I see plainly, he says, that I cannot see," as Emerson paraphrases the skeptic's cardinal joke in *Representative Men*, where Montaigne joins Luther and George Fox in an alliance of faith and self-reliance against reason.[20] The spectacle of "une science qui vise à une 'inscience,'" in the words of Alfred Glauser's *Montaigne paradoxal* (1972),[21] has comedy enough to draw the applause of that other "grand ennemi de la logique scolastique," André Gide. "Sans cesse [il] se contredit et se trahit lui-même," Gide declares in his introduction to *Les Pages immortelles de Montaigne* (1939), and he recommends this self-betrayal as exemplary to a public on the eve of a war.[22]

The suicide by studied self-contradiction pictured in the shape of the "Apologie de Raimond Sebond" gives rhetorical embodiment to the radical criticism Montaigne explicitly directs at Aristotelian reason, in both its formal underpinnings and its practical application. The traditional formal logic, he argues, requires an endless retrogression of validation, since any principle of thought must be derived from an anterior principle: "nous voylà à reculons jusques à l'infiny." The validation of practical reason is similarly endless: "Pour juger des apparences que nous recevons des subjets, il nous faudroit un instrument judicatoire; pour verifier cet instrument, il nous y faut de la demonstration; pour verifier la demonstration, un instrument: nous voilà au rouet" (2.12.265). All mortality is bound to the rack of vicious circling: "Nous roüons sans cesse en ce cercle" (2.13.273). In the place of Aristotelian logic, Montaigne sets a principle of relexive irony that is validated by its self-contradiction and which consequently does not belie the circularity and absurdity of human thought and feeling. "Il n'y a raison qui n'en aye une contraire," drawn from Sextus Empiricus, allows Montaigne to balance contraries by a roundabout logic: $-A$ balances $+A$, $+A$ balances $-A$, *ad infinitum* (2.15.276). For the principle of noncontradiction, upon which traditional *scientia* rests, he substitutes the balance of contraries, which "displays the embodied tension of living" or "the human reversibility of truth and falsity, pleasure and pain, virtue and vice."[23]

In a world of balanced opposites, all knowledge is relative or ironic. Going round and round on the circle of unreason doubling the circle of reason as charted by Montaigne, man cannot escape "le dizziquilibre" of a fever, to use Réjean Ducharme's witty bilingual coinage.[24] "Nous ne sommes jamais sans maladie. Les fièvres ont leur chaud et leur froid," as Montaigne writes (2.12.234) and Pascal copies.[25] What appears from one point of vantage as fire may appear as ice from another: "ce que nous donnons au feu, ils le donnent au froid"

(2.12.240); "le feu se picque à l'assistance du froid" (2.15.276). As with hot and cold, so with black and white. The "neige . . . noire" of Anaxagoras figures the coincidence of learning and ignorance in the sage—or the paradox of a philosophy that locates wisdom in the knowledge that nothing can be known. "Que sçay-je?" but the truth obscurely visualized in the oxymoron of dark light (2.12.191–93). Since "il y en peut avoir cent contraires autour d'un mesme subject" (2.12.230), what secular sages have to say is necessarily untrustworthy and unsound. Lame, blind, and fever-ridden, as Montaigne repeats, they speak haltingly, darkly, and deliriously, by self-contradiction.

Joining himself to all the thinkers, poets, and seers he calls up before him, Montaigne speculates that he cannot pass beyond the certainty that certain knowledge is beyond the reach of man, since the cognitive faculty, "nostre penser," is, perhaps, but "un autre songer" (2.12.261). The world and all who inhabit it constitute an element that is like a dream in its circular unreason. By Montaigne's reading, man cannot clearly distinguish waking from sleeping, folly from wisdom, darkened as his sight cannot help but be in that universal reverie: "Nostre veillée est plus endormie que le dormir; nostre sagesse, moins sage que la folie; noz songes vallent mieux que noz discours" (2.12.233). With the ironic logic underlying being and conditioning acting and seeing, linear discourse cannot articulate the truth of the dream-life. The truth of dreams is literally unspeakable since the unequivocal language and logic of simple affirmation or simple denial cannot encompass simultaneously the reality (or illusion) of balanced contraries. "Pour moy, qui ne demande qu'à devenir plus sage . . . [les] ordonnances logiciennes et Aristoteliques ne sont pas à propos," as Montaigne justly remarks in "Des Livres" (2.10.84). And the dream that is his own book gives what articulation it can to the wisdom of "une perpetuelle confession d'ignorance" or the illumination of "une nuict eternelle," in the language of "un taire parlier" (2.12.171, 192, 121). Remote from the logic of day, the *Essais* are, in the view of Glauser, "une oeuvre crépusculaire" comparable to the *poème-silence* of the symbolists,[26] whose lyricism of negation, according to Henri Brémond's *La Poésie pure* (1926), puts into action Carlyle's "Gospel of Silence."[27]

The conception of life as a dream stated in and dramatized by the *Essais* prefigures Calderón's reading of existence in his most influential work, *La Vida es sueño* (*Life Is a Dream*), published in 1635, the year following the first translation of Montaigne into Spanish.[28] In this play of dreaming and learning, the protagonist and his antagonist are set in an obscurity where the roles of victor and victim are interchangeable, there to be disabused of the illusion that man can tell fact from dream, knowledge from ignorance. The ending of *Life Is a Dream*, the mystified Polish prince Segismundo's confession of unknowing—though something is not so, to dream it is enough—invites comparison with Montaigne's sentence:

> Ceux qui ont apparié nostre vie à un songe, ont eut de la raison.
>
> Ce sont tousjours tenebres, et tenebres Cymmerienes. Nous veillons dormans, et veillans dormons.
>
> Nostre raison et nostre ame, recevant les fantasies et opinions qui luy naissent en dormant, et authorisant les actions de nos songes de pareille approbation qu'elle faict celles du jour, pourquoy ne mettons nous en doubte si nostre penser, nostre agir, n'est pas un autre songer et nostre veiller quelque espece de dormir? (*Essais* 2.12.261)

For Calderón as for Montaigne, man is a sleepwalker, a "living corpse" (*vivo cadaver*) whose immersion in the dream-life deprives him of reason and speech (*el humano discurso priva*), and whose circumambulations trace the logic ruling that ambience, where "fire and ice" (*fuego y hielo*) unite.[29] If existence is a dream, who can say for certain whether life is life or life is death? Montaigne, too, puzzles before the spectacle of a Cimmerian world, figuring it as an alliance of opposites similarly mystifying to surface reason, of black snow (2.12.191). His reason blinded, the dreamer wanders in circles; his speech made halt, he voices his ignorance in a language of privation, "the idiom of silence . . . like that of a symbolist poet."[30]

Calderón, like Montaigne, attests to the artist's solidarity with sleepwalking humanity. Basic to his works, writes Robert Ter Horst, is "the beautiful irony" of erecting "monuments to speechlessness" in words and of articulating a philosophy by "an anti-philosophy."[31] The long-sleeping Montaigne's self-diagnosis is apposite: "il . . . produit contre soy mesmes le tesmoisgnage" (2.16.286). As proposed by Schopenhauer's *The World as Will and Idea*, itself a dreamy book faithful to the contradictory logic of Montaigne as it argues and writes that action is vanity and reason groundless, *Life Is a Dream* advances the cause of enlightenment by corroborating the insight of the *Essais* and Shakespeare's *The Tempest*, that "life and dreams are leaves from the same book," a reality imperceptible to minds blinkered by "the Aristotelian logic" of "the dreary middle ages."[32] Much as it may serve to awaken by the brilliance of its insight, however, the illumination provided by the art of Montaigne and Calderón reveals, according to the suggestion of more recent students, an obscurity no less impenetrable than the unknowing made available to readers of Nicholas of Cusa's *De docta ignorantia* (*Of Learned Ignorance*), the 1566 edition of which Montaigne had within arm's reach in his tower.[33] Anticipated by the reflexive mode of argument practiced by the skeptics of antiquity against the dogmatists, Cusa rejects the principle of noncontradiction in favor of the *coincidentia oppositorum*, the logic of the infinite reconciling all differences and antinomies.[34] The Cusan principle is justly fitted to the work of Renaissance seers confronted with the opacity and unreason at the heart of things and themselves, the truth of which it is their calling to see and render. Represented on the stage of Calderón and Shakespeare, as Jackson I. Cope illustrates in *The Theater and the Dream* (1973),[35] and turned over continuously in the convoluted meditations of the *Essais*, where "les contraires se rejoignent," in the words of Jean Rousset's *Circé et le paon: la littérature de l'âge baroque en France* (1954),[36] the "coincidence of opposites" aptly formulates the grammar of an enlightenment that reckons itself ignorant and of an art that mirrors the truth it reflects by undoing itself.

While complex and at times indirect, when considered in terms of parallels, the journey from the baroque logic of "l'ignorance . . . savante" (*Essais* 1.54.370) to the speculative literature in which Emerson and Carlyle were immersed is clear enough in its broad historical lines and argument. The contribution of the *Essais*, and the "Apologie de Raimond Sebond" in particular, to the rise of synthetic idealism and the decline of analytical reason in the nineteenth century is amply illustrated in Dédéyan's study, which also notes Montaigne's "infiltration" of romantic psychology and aesthetics by way of Hume.[37] The mind's self-interrogation according to a logic of contradiction in Hume's *Enquiry concerning Human Understanding* (1748) and the subversion of rational theology in his *Dialogues concerning Natural Religion* (1779) were received as exemplary by Johann Georg Hamann,[38] for example, arguably the eighteenth century's most dedicated student of Cusa's *coincidentia oppositorum*,[39] and, as Schopenhauer recalls in the last few pages of *The World as Will and Idea*, a principal mentor to Kant and Schelling.[40] And twentieth-century sightings of Cusa's treatise of learned ignorance in the *Critique of Pure Reason* (1781) and the *System of Transcendental Idealism* (1800)[41] analogically confirm the efficacy of Hamann as an intermediary and a tutor of "philosophical ignorance."[42]

Hume's full commitment to subjectivity and its inherently reflexive mode of inquiry, a working out of Montaigne's postulate that "every affirmation involves a contradiction" since "every proposition *implies* the existence of its opposite,"[43] understandably held a powerful appeal for minds committed to undoing the separations and dualisms worked by finite logic. Calderón's metaphysical drama, acclaimed by a host of nineteenth-century German littérateurs, including Goethe, E. T. A. Hoffmann, and J. K. F. Rosencrantz, similarly assisted in that enterprise:[44] by seeing truth and illusion, matter and idea, as reversed images of each other, the author of *Life Is a Dream* had solved the enigma of the universe, his translator August Wilhelm Schlegel went so far as to claim.[45] The apotheosis of Calderón's art by German idealists rested, so Henry Sullivan's extensive documentation of its reception concludes,[46] on the conviction of finite reason's impotence before endless reality and of the comprehensive power of the limitless imagination, the faculty which, according to Coleridge's translation of Schelling, "reveals itself in the balance or reconciliation of opposite or discordant qualities."[47] Nicholas of Cusa had conceived of that faculty's power to unify in much the same terms. "You must regard the centre and the poles as coincident, using the help of your imagination as much as possible," *Of Learned Ignorance* counsels the mind which would see into the unfathomable truth of infinite being.[48]

Carlyle's "The Hero as Poet" (1840) attests to his accord with such counsel. Citing Coleridge and August Wilhelm Schlegel in confirmation, Carlyle pronounces imagination "the faculty which enables him [the poet] to discern the inner harmony" at "the centre of Being" (*On Heroes*, 337, 325). Pole rhymes with pole at "the innermost heart" of all that exists, which "inward harmony of coherence" only the imagination's "*musical* thought"[49] can comprehend and see and only the poet's song, "a kind of inarticulate unfathomable speech," can express (316). Because he sets nature and man before us "in their round completeness"—"all rounds itself off, into a kind of rhythmic coherence" in Dante and Shakespeare, Carlyle emphasizes—the poet is unmatched for the veracity of his insight (337, 341). In the words of *Sartor Resartus*, poetry is the "Music of Wisdom" (198). "A vortex, or musical tornado" in sympathetic resonance with the rhyme of opposites sounding out the universal grammar of unity, as Emerson repeats, "the all wise music" of the poet shows him "a true logician."[50] He sees integrally and speaks a "mute music."[51] Montaigne, praised by Carlyle in 1820 for his "deep insight into the principles of our common nature" and his "faithful delineation of human feelings in all their strength and weakness . . . , a mirror to every mind capable of self-examination,"[52] had meditated along much the same lines: poetry is a *discordia concors*, a music composed, "comme l'harmonie du monde, de choses contraires," of the opposites "consubstantiels à nostre vie"; and his own work he had seen as a playing of the lyre (3.13.300, 328). The comparable accounts of imagination's synthetic logic lend substance to Emerson's cryptic observation that "Carlyle is of Montaigne's opinion concerning poetry."[53] In this matter at least and in principle, the Renaissance skeptic reckoned wise by Emerson for his "Doctoral ignorance"[54] agrees with "The Hero as Poet": the most comprehensive, and therefore the least unveridical, form of thought is the poetical, the musical, the circular, the imaginative. Nor is the Montaigne-Carlyle correspondence in fundamentals limited to statement. The imagination at work in *Sartor Resartus* (1833–34), first made public by *Fraser's Magazine* in instalments begun, by coincidence, on the tricentennial of Montaigne's birth, extends the correspondence into practice.

"By way of curiosity," an 1834 reviewer of *Sartor Resartus: The Life and Opinions of Herr Teufelsdröckh,* a person, evidently, of plain sense, announces the discovery of a sentence there "which may be read either backwards or forwards."[55] The bemused reviewer is as perspicacious as he is entertaining, for *Sartor Resartus* takes the reader on a circular odyssey plotting the action and progress of the Carlylean imagination. Being a "Poetic Creation," in its own words, the book is necessarily ironic in construction and tone (201). Everything has "two meanings" in Carlyle's poem "dark with excess of bright," the reader of which, like Professor Diogenes Teufelsdröckh before a whirligig universe, is drawn "two ways at once," jerked "to and fro, in minute incessant fluctuation" analogous to the cosmic flux and reflux that *Sartor Resartus* strives faithfully to imitate (49, 79, 18). Carlyle's is a feverish text, blowing hot and cold in rhythm with the universal "fever-paroxysms" mirrored in the poetical metaphysician's enigmatic life and his no less baffling opinions (87, 119, 121). The "delirious vertigo" (130) produced in the Editor as reader of the Professor's biography and thought, both true to the logic of the creation figured in the complex of images central to *Sartor Resartus*— not of clothes, but of tornadoes, eddies, whirlpools within whirlpools, whirlwinds, wheels within wheels, vortices, and spinning tops—describes as well the effect of Carlyle's own book, itself a work of labyrinthine tortuosities generated by the "revolutions" or "circulations" holding universal sway (7, 14, 78). *Sartor Resartus* is an infinite "circumambulation" (113), literally an "eccentricity," to use Emerson's substantive for the work's genius in the preface to the New England edition of 1836.[56]

Spun from the bedevilments attendant on graphing the life of a mind given to "quaint tricksy turns," habitually going "to and fro" (22, 18), Carlyle's fictional psycho-biography represents the work of an imagination cognate with Montaigne's. As Montaigne describes "[l']irresolution infinie" of his roundabout divagations, "Je ne fay qu'aller et venir" (2.12.226, 231). "Un ensemble qui forme un cercle," according to the configuration drawn by Michel Butor's *Essais sur les Essais* (1968),[57] the skeptic's mercurial art has neither beginning nor end, like "un serpent qui se mord la queue," in the eyes of a more recent commentator.[58] The reader who would follow the mind's journey that Montaigne's book recounts is compelled to do likewise, of course, "à revenir en arrière" with each step forward in the *Essais*.[59] And so it is with readers of *Sartor Resartus*, who must proceed by the light of imaginative rather than linear thinking as they wend their way along the gyrations of the "Serpent-of-Eternity" (*Sartor*, 153) traced by the book. The serpentine logic of the imagination, like the infinite dream-thinking celebrated for its power to reconcile opposites in Novalis's *Hymns to the Night* (1800), is designed to charm the reader experiencing its sinuosities into accepting the unifying embrace extended by Carlyle's fiction. "It is certain my Belief gains quite *infinitely* the moment I can convince another mind thereof," *Sartor Resartus* translates Novalis (161). The fundamental conviction, shared by Montaigne as well, is repeated in *Lord Jim*, Conrad's fiction of "the intimate alliance of contradictions"[60] taking a later translation of that dictum for its epigraph: "Nature" is "the balance of colossal forces," "the mighty Kosmos in perfect equilibrium," pronounces Stein, the philosopher of infinity and dreams who provides Marlow with nighttime tuition.[61] *Sartor Resartus* strives to simulate just such a balance, with the least avoidable injustice. The maker of its "Night-thoughts" (*Sartor*, 16), accordingly, takes for his guide and ruling principle the imagination, the inconclusive and mercurial "roundabout logic of emotions."[62]

Sartor Resartus gives rhetorical embodiment to the philosophy of balanced contraries accented with a special ardor by nineteenth-century German idealists. "Carlyle always begins with a contradiction," writes Emerson.[63] And this is certainly the case in *Sartor Resartus*, which begins in two discordant voices: the Editor, an agent of sense with an aversion to traveling in circles, enters into conflict and communion with Diogenes Teufelsdröckh, a philosopher of the imagination. The "aimless discontinuity" (121) and "eye-bewildering *chiaroscuro*" (140) of Teufelsdröckh's interminable discoursing make it intractable stuff to the Editor hungry for logical coherence and unambiguous light. But the differences separating the biographer from his subject are not insurmountable, and the very act of composition gradually trains him to the truth of the Professor's axiom: "Not our Logical, Mensurative faculty, but our Imaginative one is King over us" (166). The voice of the imaginative faculty prevails over the mensurative in the end; and the Editor comes to transcend his differences with Teufelsdröckh, to rise, according to Jerry A. Dibble's *The Pythia's Drunken Song* (1978), to "a higher state of consciousness which contains and cancels all opposition."[64] Thanks to the bumpers of poetical reasoning imbibed with the mystic Professor-of-Things-in-General, his mystified biographer it at last able to see eye to eye with the double-thinking mind he sings. The aesthetic reconciliation so achieved analogically answers to the unitary reality of Teufelsdröckh's life and works, and allegorically sustains the moral imperative which his poetico-philosophical insight is said to generate. This much, on the face of it, is certain in Carlyle: "love God. This is the EVERLASTING YEA, wherein all contradiction is solved" (145).

By Teufelsdröckh's—and Carlyle's—own logic, however, the EVERLASTING YEA is no unequivocal solution to the conflict of opposites. As with the *Essais*, the balance of contraries in true knowing or learned ignorance advanced by and practiced in *Sartor Resartus* cannot avoid being governed by the circular logic of relativity. The voice of Teufelsdröckh, striving to articulate "the inarticulate mystic speech of Music," acknowledges that "spiritual music can spring only from discords set in harmony;... but for Evil there were no Good" (110, 97). Carlyle's philosopher comes close to translating Montaigne's reflection on music's loving work:

> Nostre vie est composée, comme l'harmonie du monde, de choses contraires.... Le musicien qui n'en aymeroit que les uns, que voudroit il dire? Il faut qu'il s'en sçache servir en commun et les mesler. Et nous aussi, les biens et les maux, qui sont consubstantiels à nostre vie. (3.13.300)

Since it is a harmonizing of contraries—of "Infinite and Finite; Relative and Absolute; Apparent and Real," in the words of Emerson's "Montaigne; or, The Sceptic"[65]—what the musician sings is a counterpoint no more or less ambiguous than the love that *Sartor Resartus* figures as "a Delirium... a discerning of the Infinite in the Finite, of the Idea made Real; which discerning again may be either true or false, either seraphic or demoniac, Inspiration or Insanity" (109). The "delirious vertigo in his thought" shows Teufelsdröckh a bona fide agent of unreason, a lover and musician. As Carlyle's vortical thinker who experiences a duel of opposing forces during an arctic June night observes, "Fire-whirlwind, Creation and Destruction proceed together" in "the Bedlam of Creation," a place of "mad loves and mad hatreds... farce-tragedy, beast-godhood" (135, 182–83). Faithful to the logic of the inscrutable existence its musical thinking would render, Carlyle's own literary composition is inherently two-faced, like the coin Emerson sees Montaigne flipping and spinning throughout the *Essais*. It is a "Bag of Doubloons" (*Sartor*, 19–20).

Symbols, in the view of Carlyle the only positive means available for the expression of the truth beyond reason, also share in the irony of being and seeing. It is, as *Sartor Resartus* announces, by symbol's agency that "the Infinite is made to blend itself with the Finite" and that the artist is able to voice "the inarticulate mystic speech of Music" (165, 110). Just as irony is the mode that the two-sidedness of existence compels philosophers such as Hume to adopt,[66] so is the use of symbol commanded to the Carlylean artist taxed with telling the conundrum of coinciding opposites. Symbols serve "to suggest either a complex of discordant ideas or a fundamental harmony between apparent discords," according to Barbara Seward's refashioning of Carlyle's account in *Sartor Resartus*.[67] Coined to embody the skeptic's inveterate double-thinking and double-speaking, the literary symbol is an ironic device that takes in opposites together in a single comprehension.

The way of the symbolist and the metaphysical ironist, so inviting to the mind that would see things whole, is not without peril, however. Sometimes, an ironic turn of mind may take the speculator to the point farthest removed from the one he had intended to reach. Montaigne had not altogether avoided that danger. In his quest for sure and balanced knowledge, he had sought to discover everything in himself, yet had found, in addition to doubt, a bottomless void. As he confesses following a meditation on Ovid's Narcissus, "je ne pouvoy souffrir la veuë de cette profondeur infinie sans horreur." Montaigne's gazing into the bottomless self has led in this instance to a kind of hell: he reads in the mirror of the Ovidian fable of endless and futile self-pursuit the lineaments of a mind that burns with the fire it lights (2.12.259). Teufelsdröckh is similarly horrified by the spectacle of an "Infernal Chase" of the self after the self and of a heart devouring itself in solitude (120, 125), preludes to the vision of nothingness accorded the philosopher as he gazes into the mirror of "the Infinite Brine" on an arctic June midnight: opposite forces clash, whirl about, and annihilate each other (135–37). Kenneth Burke's *Language as Symbolic Action* (1968) appropriately terms this a "Zero Moment," when plus and minus cancel out each other, leaving an infernal void, the EVERLASTING NO.[68]

The Zero Moment is a logical outcome of Carlyle's reflexive thinking, as the editor of the Temple Edition of Dante's *Inferno* implies when he cites the EVERLASTING NO in his commentary on Canto 34, where fire and ice unite, and Satan, in the words of Burke, "cancels himself, as the beating of his wings . . . sends forth draughts that freeze him all the more."[69] Here is imaged, ironically enough, the negative philosophy of reconciliation able to take simultaneously into account the EVERLASTING NO, repudiated by Carlyle, and the EVERLASTING YEA, which he affirms. "In Equivocal Worlds, Up & Down are Equivocal," Blake serves to remind.[70] The EVERLASTING YEA and the EVERLASTING NO are married by the synthetic logic at work in "the innermost frozen circle of Dante's Inferno," in the language of Conrad's "The Warrior's soul."[71] Like the Professor's life and the universe or "Great World-Serpent . . . tail in mouth" (*On Heroes*, 274) it mirrors, Carlyle's fiction is a tangle of double-thinking with head inseparable from tail, a "pitcher of tamed vipers" or an "unspeakable hurly-burly" with a devilish tumbler in motley for its presiding genius (*Sartor*, 16, 73). A scientist of the imagination able to endorse "the incompatibility absolute" between Heaven and Hell, light and darkness in Dante even as he extols the medieval poet's "unfathomable" mystic song of "fiery snow" for its depth and integrity in "The Hero as Poet" (329, 331, 325), Carlyle ever retraces the circle of hellish unreason that the harlequin's whirling antics have always spun. As A. Abbott Ikeler, taking Emerson's reading of Carlylean self-contradiction as a significant indicator, demonstrates, even the celebrated dogmatist of the later works remains divided in his loyalties. He never quite succeeds in putting behind him that allegiance to those infernal poetic sports practiced in *Sartor Resartus* and which he comes with increasing emphasis, though inconstantly, to abjure.[72]

Carlyle, then, has cause to see himself as a writer of "paper-whirlpools" struggling to keep his head "above water . . . amid infinite contradictions."[73] Ostensibly written not only to depict for the doubters and unbelievers of his generation "the far-reaching consequences of their pessimism but also to make plain to them their true path out of it," by W. H. Hudson's reckoning in 1908,[74] *Sartor Resartus* makes nothing plain in fact and recommends, if anything, adoption of the skeptic's negative way. What truth Carlyle's Socratic "dialectic marauder" Teufelsdröckh reads in the world (*Sartor*, 108), Montaigne, Hume, and Schopenhauer confirm: "This Dreaming, this Somnambulism is what we on Earth call Life; wherein the most indeed undoubtingly wander, as if they knew right hand from left; yet they only are wise who know that they know nothing" (40). Nor does the chapter "Natural Supernaturalism," the culmination of *Sartor Resartus* and of Carlyle's "whole spiritual life,"[75] dispel the darkness of such know-nothingism. Consisting mainly of questions—close to four dozen of them—"Natural Supernaturalism" ends with Carlyle's favorite passage from Shakespeare:

> we are such stuff
> As dreams are made of; and our little life
> Is rounded with a sleep.
> *(The Tempest* 1.2)

A profession of the reality of illusion wraps up a tangle of unanswered questions. And the ironic discourse of the dream metaphor here expressing Carlyle's theme of unknowing speaks the syntax of the book as a whole. *Sartor Resartus* is a somnambulist's creation, illustrating the power of dream and symbol as formulated by the nineteenth-century aesthetician Henri-Frédéric Amiel: "cette puissance du rêve de fondre ensemble les incompatibles, d'unir ce qui s'exclût, d'identifier le oui et le non."[76] The dreamer-artist's path of enlightenment and reconciliation leads to the learned ignorance which the skeptic finally reaches: with "le mariage des contraires" in dreams comes "la sagesse folle."[77] Who is to know anything but the truth of ignorance and obscurity in the life of unreason, dream, and symbol? What *is* certain is that there is no telling right hand from left in *Sartor Resartus*. Carlyle's creation is well within the bounds of art set by Wilde's epigram: "A Truth in art is that whose contradictory is also true."[78]

Another peril waiting on Carlyle as an artist of coinciding opposites is indifference, a state of mind that, like the EVERLASTING NO, he frequently and vehemently assailed. And yet, it is a state of mind he could not altogether avoid, having chosen the way of the symbolist, the metaphysical ironist, and the romantic mystic. *Sartor Resartus* locates all three in "a vague, gray half-light," the middle region between "Death and Life," "the Everlasting Night" and "the Everlasting Day" (55, 116, 64). As Carlyle's fiction emphatically repeats, theirs is an experience of the "heavenly attraction" of opposite valences: they dwell in suspension, "as between Negative and Positive" (101–2). "The Centre of Indifference," midway between opposite poles, seems an appropriate place to find a logician of the balancing imagination. There is in the symbol-speaker Teufelsdröckh "a natural diabolico-angelical Indifference" (177). He shares the vision of the model metaphysician in Carlyle's essay on Geothe, who sees humanity suspended in a great tension: "Everywhere the human soul stands between a hemisphere of light and another of darkness."[79]

In the words of *Sartor Resartus,* "the Philosopher" who would see the whole truth of things as they are "must station himself in the middle" (50), the position taken by Montaigne, whose *Essais,* like Carlyle's philosophical poem, sets the reader in a twilight world: "Il peint . . . tout en gris, ce qui est sa teinte naturelle."[80]

But there is also discord between Carlyle and Montaigne. True to his principle of the relativity of knowing, of "discords set in harmony," Carlyle occasionally reverses his perspective, to see with the eyes of the traditional Western logician. And justifiably so, since a logic that denies the principle of noncontradiciton can raise no valid objection to a way of thinking set against it. "Tous leurs principes sont vrais," as Pascal turns skepticism back on the skeptics, "mais leurs conclusions sont fausses, parce que les principes opposés sont vrais aussi."[81] The relativist Conrad writes to the same effect in *Under Western Eyes:* "A train of thought is never false."[82] In 1820, Carlyle published this criticism of Montaigne: "On contemplating this picture [of himself], we are surprised to find the principles of a stoic incongruously mingled with the practice of an epicure."[83] More surprising, perhaps, is that Carlyle should have been surprised by contradiction in a writer who explains that what appears as fire from one point of vantage may appear as ice from another. His criticism of Montaigne, significantly, parallels the commentary of Dugald Stewart, a major spokesman for the late eighteenth-century Philosophy of Common Sense raised to defend science against skepticism, Hume's in particular. Stewart remarks "the strange and apparently inconsistent combination of knowledge and ignorance which the writings of Montaigne exhibit. . . . [He] argues, at different times . . . on opposite sides of the same question."[84] At bottom, what Stewart and Carlyle find perplexing is Montaigne's indifference, his rejection of linear thought in favor of a contradictory logic of balance. A habitual practitioner of just such a logic himself,[85] Carlyle takes aim at himself in his Montaigne article, and thereby ironically confirms that the *Essais*'s "faithful delineation of human feelings in all their strength and weakness, will serve as a mirror to every mind capable of self-examination."[86] The Carlylean dialectic, too, leads to a suspension between contraries; and, like Montaigne's thought, suicidal in its practice of contradiction, it must allow the equal truth or falsehood of its antithesis, of a positive philosophy grounded on the principle of noncontradiction. The conflict between Carlyle and Montaigne follows from their agreement on the principle of the *discordia concors.* Their discord follows from their harmony.

The unlimited freedom that unreason confers is, in the final account, the likely cause of the dissonance in the harmony between Montaigne and Carlyle. In the absence of reason, man is free to choose whatever faith he will; in a "universe of Nescience" (*Sartor*, 172), to erect belief on doubt. Montaigne, on the one hand, chooses to accept Roman Catholicism as authoritative in matters of faith and morals and dies a son of the Church. Carlyle, on the other hand, reflects a theological creed raised, in part, in protest against Montaigne's. Once a pilgrim to Montaigne's chateau in Périgord, there to copy inscriptions from the library walls, John Sterling, a close friend (and antagonist) of Carlyle, ends an 1838 article with a comparison of the English philosopher of vortices with Luther.[87] The comparison, emphasized by Harris in 1978, is also suggested by Paul Claudel's observation, that Goethe's *Faust*, a major source for *Sartor Resartus*, dramatizes the anti-Aristotelian creed of Luther.[88] The diabolico-angelical Teufelsdröckh, like his creator, reads Luther's version of the Bible. As Nathalie Haldin reflects in Conrad's tale of "Eastern logic" unrolled "under . . . Western eyes," the world is not governed by "the strict logic of ideas," a pronouncement that the ostensibly rational Westerner, the English Teacher, like the Editor at the beginning of *Sartor Resartus*, cannot divine since he is unable to see how "antagonistic ideas" are "to be reconciled."[89] Coincident in the science of unknowing, Montaigne's and Carlyle's thought lead them to conflicting convictions. The skeptic has the last word: *par mesme voye une croyance contraire*.

Carlyle's "unspeaking" before Montaigne shows the "Gospel of Silence" in action. "Speech is of Time, Silence is of Eternity," as *Sartor Resartus* avers (164). For Carlyle, silence is the precise negative expression of humanity's nescience before the infinity of the self and the world, where opposites coincide. Simply literal, finite language, with its linear syntax, is speechless in the face of infinite reality. There is also, Carlyle explains by the voice of Teufelsdröckh, a positive way of saying the unsayable, by symbol, the instrument for the reconciliation of disparate or opposite elements: "In a Symbol there is concealment and yet revelation; here therefore, by Silence and by Speech acting together, comes a double significance" (165). By the symbol's reflexive grammar, "Like-Unlike" are harmonized (102) and "the Infinite is made to blend itself with the Finite" (165). As this essay has proposed, Montaigne and Carlyle are both like and unlike, their disagreement extending from their agreement in the dreamy logic of learned ignorance. Perhaps Carlyle perceived not only the "great deep cleft" dividing them but also "the rock-strata, miles deep," where their "two poor souls are at one," and sensed that, from his point of vantage at least, the only positive way of uttering the whole truth of his ironic relationship with Montaigne was by symbol. Straight discourse would not have proved up to the task. The double-thinking lover of wisdom whom Emerson likened to Mephistopheles and Montaigne in May 1834[90] chose instead the negative way, to remain silent.

2
Emerson's Divine Comedy

> Nous avons les yeux plus grands que le ventre.
> —Montaigne, "Des cannibales"

> The inner truth is hidden—luckily, luckily.
> —Conrad, *Heart of Darkness*

"CARLYLE has led us into the desert, and he has left us there."[1] So Arthur Hugh Clough lamented to Emerson on 15 July 1848 as they walked the deck of the new Royal Mail steamer *Europa* preparing to depart Liverpool for Boston. With the departure of the Sage of Concord the idealistic young men of England would be left without a teacher and guide. Emerson, it seems, found a justness in that figure, of Carlyle as a Moses deserting his followers at the moment they most needed his leadership, an image all the more telling for the middle-aged American's tacit confidence in the *Europa*'s captain to navigate "the awful desert [of the Atlantic] in which no caravan loiters."[2]

Journal entries for 1847–48 suggest why he agreed with Clough. "I find C[arlyle] always cunning," Emerson complained. "He denies the books he reads . . . denies his own acts & purposes;—By God, I do not know them—and immediately the cock crows" (*JMN* 10:338).[3] Carlyle finds "intolerable" in a speaker "the twist that was in every thing he said" (*JMN* 10:343), even though he himself is just such a speaker. Those who go to him for enlightenment or direction are consequently reduced to despair: "They all feel the caprice and variety" in the opinions of this "covenanter-philosopher & . . . sansculotte-aristocrat" (*JMN* 10:261, 550). Carlyle is a patchwork of contradictions, something of a devilish jester. "It is droll to hear this talker talking against talkers, and this writer writing against writing," Emerson thought to himself in February 1848 (*JMN* 10:232), confirming John Sterling's earlier diagnosis of a suicidal logic in Carlyle's writings, of "all manner of random and amorphous assertions [which]

... like bursting cannon and reverting Congreve-rockets, injure his own cause...."[4] By contrast, Emerson sees himself as a man who cares for one kind of talk only, "short plain dealing" (*JMN* 11:60). In May 1834, after reading four installments of *Sartor Resartus,* Emerson had counseled his friend to despise "the charm of diabolism," that "Mephistophelism" reveling in grotesque humor and the antics of topsy-turvydom,[5] which criticism is to resurface in a journal entry some three decades later: "Carlyle's humour & daemonic fun" abuse "the whole world as mad dunces," including his own heroes and himself (*JMN* 15:476). Clearly, Carlyle had not taken Emerson's advice to follow in the way of sobriety, and was consequently unfit to serve as leader. Not long after his return to New England in 1848, Emerson observed of a man who "shifts his purpose nimbly," that he suffers from "the same vice" for which a Boston pilot was stripped of his certificate of competence (*JMN* 11:54).[6]

Serious as it is in the strictures against Carlyle it implies and sums up, Emerson's compliance with Clough has something of the comical in it, for it involves an act of self-reflection true to Montaigne's principle, that "the self is the sole subject we study & learn" (*JMN* 4:68). The "imperial muse" of the great poet and teacher, faithful to "any caprice of thought," plays with the universe as with "a bauble," Emerson exhorts and proclaims in *Nature* (1836).[7] "Self-Reliance," in *Essays: First Series* (1841), adds forgetfulness as an aid to such fidelity. If a man remembers what he said yesterday, he may be tempted to honor it today, when his feelings or convictions have changed. "With consistency a great soul has simply nothing to do" (*W* 2:57). And *Society and Solitude* (1870), though more temperately in view of the limitations taught by long experience, continues to invest the poet and orator with the "daemoniacal power" of the despotic Pied Piper of Hamelin, to make the world dance to his tune, "make day out of night" (*W* 7:93, 65, 161). "L'état, c'est Moi," first entered in Emerson's journal in 1824 (*JMN* 2:211), continues as the emperor poet's motto.

Emerson confirmed his teachings by his practice, much to the delight or frustration of his public, as the history of their responses shows. By Kenneth Marc Harris's reckoning in 1978, Emerson studies show that "evidence can always be found to contradict the most carefully considered conclusions."[8] More recent warnings to the reader, pointing to the bafflement and giddiness that the rapid succession of persons and personae,[9] matters and styles,[10] in Emerson's writing must produce, sustain that observation, thereby seconding the advisories issued in 1861 to those who might enter the "labyrinth" of *The Conduct of Life* (1860) in search of unequivocal precepts:

"EMERSON never had a fixed opinion about anything."[11] This is the educator of quicksilver-like virtue acknowledged by Henry Ketcham as "a leader of leaders, a teacher of teachers" in 1887[12] and cited shortly thereafter by an aesthete looking to authorize the iron jurisdiction of unreason in affairs of art and civic tuition: "Who wants to be consistent? [. . .] Not I. Like Emerson, I write over the door of my library the word 'Whim' "—so a musician in Oscar Wilde's *Intentions* (1891) merrily justifies his writing of an article intended to be useful to the public.[13] In the same dialogue, "The Decay of Lying," Carlyle's *French Revolution* (1837) shares in the praise of caprice: it shows the "superb irresponsibility" of "the true liar."[14] As sympathetically, though in a less earnestly playful way, Dorothy Richardson's *Pilgrimage* (1938) locates Emerson and Carlyle among those Victorian sages who, "professing thought and its expression to be secondary activities, had nevertheless spent their lives thinking and setting down their thoughts."[15] And the logic of self-contradiction has been detected in the substance of that thought as well. "His fundamental position is, the good of evil," according to a bewildered Sterling's summary of Carlylean doctrine,[16] which same sentence is underscored in Melville's copy of *The Conduct of Life*, with a comment suggestive of his exasperation with what he evidently takes to be its willful, characteristically Emersonian flaunting of opposed orders of value: Emerson "still bethinks himself of his Optimism—he must make that good somehow against the eternal hell itself."[17]

But Emerson's puzzled readers did not tell him very much he did not already know. Long before Melville's purchase of *The Conduct of Life* in November 1870, Emerson had generalized from an extended observation of his own fluxions during a sea voyage to Rome in search of "the Master" (*L* 1:376), that "the weathercock is the wisest man" (*JMN* 4:105). Afloat on the Mediterranean in January 1833, he had attempted to learn the use of the quadrant from the ship's master, a man worth "a thousand philosophers" for what he knows; but every day Emerson had displayed "a more astounding ignorance" (*JMN* 4:107, 115). Having failed "to learn in sunshine" how to get a fix on his position, he had "comforted himself at midnight" by reading Milton's *Lycidas* in the privacy of his cabin (*JMN* 4:110–11). Emerson was not to find the Master, "that wise man whom everywhere I seek" (*L* 1:374), in Rome, but he did meet there a man whose letter of introduction helped open the way to Craigenputtock Farm and Carlyle,[18] who was eventually to show himself as qualified as the drifting quester from New England to fill the role of master. "I met myself," Emerson remembered in 1849 (*JMN* 11:101), giving the truth of experience to the prediction he had made some three years before boarding the *Europa:* "A pilgrim wandering in search of a man. This too will be a looking-glass business" (*JMN* 9:206). The weathercock pilgrim and the capricious Carlyle made a good match. Sidney Lanier's puckish comment on the service of his fellow countryman provides a measure of that similitude's justness: "He took me by the hand and led me nowhere. . . ."[19] "I float drifting far & wide . . . without port without chart," as Emerson himself pictures his mental traveling (*L* 2:175).[20]

There is cause, then, to detect at least a trace of laughter in Emerson's voice as it speaks in this journal entry of 1861: "I often think I could write a criticism on Emerson, that would hit the white" (*JMN* 15:113). He had already done so, by a reading of himself in the mirror of Carlyle. And he would do so again, in criticism of the kind his venerable teacher Plotinus practiced to telling effect in an attack on Heraclitus for engaging in metaphor and the logic of coinciding opposites, and consequently setting his students adrift in mystery, without the least explanation for a guide.[21] As Henry Demarest Lloyd recalled in 1896, "Emerson had that love of fun, that insight into the absurd. [. . .] He did not spare himself. He did not spare his own craft."[22] Certainly, "the story" of the Emerson-Carlyle correspondence is "a Plutarchian one," of "high and low, hot and cold, dark and light," as Joseph Slater aptly summarizes,[23] though it would be more comprehensive to speak of not one story but two, and of both as soliloquies, with each protagonist "self-centered" like Montaigne, according to Emerson's comparison in a letter to Carlyle,[24] each engaged in "internecine work," in the words of a Carlyle letter to Emerson.[25] "A Plotinus-Montaigne" in the eyes of James Russell Lowell,[26] a "teetotalling Bacchus . . . and ministerial Pan" to a more recent wit,[27] Emerson simulates the Carlylean condition, of "a figure divided against himself."[28] And it could hardly have been otherwise, given Emerson's tireless attention to his own "undulatory and alternate" pulse (*W* 3:68), listening there to the rhymes and echoes of the joyous heavenly laws of "Reaction and Recoil," which "Teach flames to freeze & ice to boil" (*JMN* 9:438; *W* 2:129, 9:14).

A slave forging his own fetters (*JMN* 2:154), an attacker annihilated by the recoil of his cannon (*W* 2:107), a fire extinguishing itself (*JMN* 9:410), a self-condemned demon torturing himself (*JMN* 12:191), a harpoon flying back at the harpooner (*EL* 3:146), a house divided against itself (*JMN* 2:251), a man biting and tearing himself (*JMN* 8:236–37), a worker cutting himself with his own tools (*JMN* 12:201), and a speaker unsaying his words as he speaks them (*JMN* 5:77)—these figures confirm Emerson as a faithfully autoscopic critic of "the Reflective Age" (*JMN* 5:366), "the age of the first person singular" (*JMN* 12:198), "the age of Suicide" (*L* 2:445). Unlike Carlyle, however, Emerson was not put out of humor by his self-inflicted wounds; nor did attacks from enemies other than himself substantially detract from his optimism for the coming age.[29] No "morbidness" for Emerson in "this Age of consciousness or introversion" (*JMN* 7:16). Quite the contrary: the cycle of "internecine war . . . pleases at a sufficient perspective" (*JMN* 13:87). Suicide, in fact, like chaos,[30] is converted to positive agency in Emerson. It is fundamental to his method as a teacher of wisdom and at the source of much of his playfulness in the practice of that vocation.

As the editor of *Emerson: Prophecy, Metamorphosis, and Influence* (1975) recognizes, there are "comical implications" in studying a mind that counsels others to take counsel only from themselves.[31] No secondhand gospel has authority to teach, Emerson always insisted. Understandably, then, the (in)efficacy of his career as a moral leader much gratified him. "I delight in driving men from me," Emerson recorded in 1859 (*JMN* 14:258), summing up some thirty years in the comic enterprise of a teacher whose best advice had been that no one trust him and whose final task was to fill out a work he sometimes called *Philosophy for the People*.[32] In this respect, Emerson recalls the Goethe Carlyle once pronounced unfit to serve as an ethical guide to others: even this, "the greatest of contemporary men . . . is not to have any follower, and should not have any."[33] He should not because his is a radically private and endlessly circular enterprise founded on the equivocating poetics of hell.[34] How, then, in the words of Melville, did Emerson make his "Optimism . . . good . . . against the eternal hell itself"?[35] How was he able to extract "milk" out of "poison" or "sunbeams" out of "darkness" (*L* 2:117), to draw utility and delight from suicidal internecine war? An exploration of that question so baffling to sense provides a way of tracking Emerson in some of the twists and turns in his mind's happy journey.

Nil fuit unquam sit dispar tibi, Emerson copied under the heading "Myself" on Sunday, 18 April 1824 (*JMN* 2:237). Never was a creature so inconsistent: hyperbolic though it may be in its application, the line from Horace's *Satires* suits him. In one mood, the recent graduate of Harvard College and schoolteacher in search of more congenial work can mourn "the scepticism of knowledge, the darkness of light"; in another, believe that "nothing is more ungrounded than the assertion that, scepticism is, in any way, the natural fruit of a superior understanding"; and in yet another, celebrate the honesty and wisdom of Socrates in affirming that he knows nothing but his own ignorance (*JMN* 2:171, 109, 319). Faithful to the injunction "Know thyself," Emerson shows a similar probity in describing himself as "a motley patchwork of feelings" (*JMN* 2:101). And it is on the basis of such self-knowledge that he hoped to build a new career in 1824. His passionate love of rhetoric and the weakness of his "reasoning faculty" give substance to his hope "in Divinity . . . to thrive." Emerson finds his temperament well adapted to flourish in the "debatable ground" that is theology, a work depending "chiefly on the imagination" (*JMN* 2:238–39). Like the reading of the "dubious theme" that is "myself," in his words of 1823 (*JMN* 2:111), that study takes the vagaries of doubt for its province, leaving the student ample room for private speculation free of the constraints of reason. For a creature of unreason gifted for rhetoric, divinity is best.

The argument from temperament which underpins the future preacher's decision to enter Harvard Divinity School yields a principle more than a match to it in piquancy. "Every man's heaven is different; and is coloured by the character," affirms a journal entry of 1823 (*JMN* 2:84). The fact that Milton's Father of Lies had found consolation and cause for optimism in such a notion gives Emerson no caution. Nor is this young student of divinity slow or reluctant explicitly to acknowledge (though only to himself) the consonance of Satan's voice with his own, as when he puts in the mouth of a philanthropist these lines from *Paradise Lost*

> The Mind is its own place, and in itself
> Can make a Heaven of Hell, a Hell of Heaven.
> What matter where, if I be still the same
>
> (1.254–56)

adding the comment: "There is no danger of any excess in the practice of this doctrine" (*JMN* 2:330). Emerson's enthusiastic endorsement of the Devil's doctrine tacitly informs his subsequent preaching as a Unitarian minister. "The world is but a mirror in which every mind sees its own image reflected," he teaches in the 1830 sermon "Self-Culture,"[36] and comes to find in that conviction a stimulus to the life of authorship. In the privacy of his room, in a resolution of 6 January 1832, the year of his resignation from the Unitarian ministry, Emerson allows the voice of the skeptical demonic *I* to speak outrightly this time: he would write a book, the first chapter to take for its ruling text, "That the mind is its own place" (*JMN* 3:316). His first book, *Nature,* published anonymously in 1836, with its chapter "Idealism," lives up to that resolve.

The voice of Milton's Satan resonant in the early formulation of Emerson's principle of subjectivity is rarely to be altogether out of hearing, thanks in part to his lifelong association with Montaigne and his analogical twinning of the author of the *Essais* with the hero of *Paradise Lost*. "Montaigne, always Montaigne. . . . What hell could be found for such—. . . converting every place into the one thing needful, & every hobgoblin into the best company . . . . The hero is always where he is"—a reflection from 1859, for example, is rewritten for *The Conduct of Life*, where Montaigne reappears in the guise of a monk who, taken to hell by an angel, makes "a kind of heaven of it" (*JMN* 14:279; *W* 6:194). Like the fallen archangel recreated by *The Marriage of Heaven and Hell*, the Emersonian Montaigne is a magus, a wonderworker able to convert a substance into its opposite in the twinkling of an eye; "the eye altering alters all," the sixty-five-year-old Emerson copies from Blake's "The Mental Traveller" (*JMN* 16:90). Accordingly, as he recalls in the preface to *Parnassus* (1874), "Montaigne is delightful in his egotism."[37] The presence of a kindred deviltry both in his own egotism and in the happiness or comedy it takes for its end is no secret to him. "I have no fears in my own despite to play . . . the devil's attorney," Emerson's lecture "Worship" makes plain in *The Conduct of Life* (*W* 6:201). His is a playful working at cross-purposes well designed to stimulate delight in the attentive understanding: in the words of "The Comic," from *Letters and Social Aims* (1876), "It affects us oddly, to see things turned upside down" (*W* 8:169). If the idealist's end is divine—"to chart an inward heaven," according to Sherman Paul's *Emerson's Angles of Vision* (1952)—[38] the means for that charting are, oddly and comically enough, those of the Shape-Shifter; and if a heaven, it is one where the merrily inconsistent agent of unreason, like the heroic Montaigne making and unmaking people and places with *la gaya scienza* of the exemplary Father of Lies, has no cause to feel *dépaysé*. As Gerald Morgan observes in his "Harlequin Faustus: Marlowe's Comedy of Hell" (1967), the "assumption of subjectivity . . . seldom allows other than hellish mirth."[39]

The devilish topsy-turvy logic underlying the light merriment of Emersonian catachresis—of birds and castles resting on clouds, and men lifting themselves up by their own ears, for example—is invaluable to him in the business of searching for a way to realize an earthly divine comedy. Sirach's maxim, "All things are double one against another" (Ecclesiasticus 33:15), frequently cited and never far from the suface of Emerson's early thought when most vexed,[40] summarizes the basis of what he takes to be the truly infernal in man's condition. "Succession, divisions, parts, particles,—this is the condition, this the tragedy of man" (*JMN* 7:105). *Ogni medaglia ha il suo riverso*, as the proverb ruefully says in Montaigne's "Des boyteux";[41] everything is unwhole and, like a coin, has "two faces," according to the figure opening Emerson's "Montaigne; or, The Sceptic," in *Representative Men* (1850) (W 4:149). There can be no heavenly comedy, no balance or reconciliation of opposite or discordant elements in a world constituted of unresolved dualities and ruled by the logic of contradiction and separation. "When will you mend Montaigne?" Emerson asked himself in May 1835: when will he "weld the finite & infinite, the absolute & seeming together," and mend the universal duplicity rendered by Sirach's sentence (*JMN* 5:40)?

Humanity awaits its physician, and not in vain. The wonderful cure, at once allo- and homeopathic, for what ails the expectant multitude will be provided by the Devil's doctrine. Montaigne, who had wound up his *Essais* with a final tweaking of philosophy with the memory of her mentor Socrates—he was never one to preach against the marriage of "le divin avec le terrestre, le raisonnable avec le desraisonnable, le severe à l'indulgent, l'honneste au deshonneste" (3.13.325)—will cure himself. As Montaigne had canonized the laughing, introspective Socrates (3.12.265), so *Representative Men* elevates "this prince of egotists" to the rank of "Saint Michel de Montaigne" (W 4:162, 173).

Nature, published sixteen months after the pressing self-interrogation of May 1835, recounts Emerson's progress in his search along the way to concord. Its sixth chapter, "Idealism," in a passage which has for its stated intention, ironically, the demonstration of "a dualism," "the difference between the observer and the spectacle," conducts a whirlwind tour designed to show the effects of perspective on the world:

> We are strangely affected by seeing the shore from a moving ship, from a balloon, or through the tints of an unusual sky. The least change in our point of view, gives the whole world a pictorial air. A man who seldom rides, needs only to get into a coach and traverse his own town, to turn the streets into a puppet-show. . . . What new thoughts are suggested by seeing a face of country quite familiar, in the rapid movement of the railroad car! . . . Turn the eyes upside down, by looking at the landscape through your legs, and how agreeable is the picture, though you have seen it any time these twenty years! (W 1:50–51)

By unfixing the world, experiences such as imagined here authorize the assumption of subjectivity and recommend the certitude of idealism. And this passage, in its own action, figures the working of the book as a whole. A paratactical array of arguments from experience and its illustrative vagaries of perspective, *Nature* strives to achieve an effect simulating that of philosophy when practiced in the mode of Hume and Berkeley. By making "mountains dance & smoke & disappear," according to Emerson in February 1836, their thought advances the cause of "Religion" among the refined (*JMN* 5:123). As the rhetorical conflation of *I, you,* and *we* in *Nature* more than suggests, the hope is that each reader will take the work as exemplary and duplicate its performance. "What's a book?" Emerson had asked himself in October 1835. It is "everything or nothing. The eye that sees it is all" (*JMN* 5:93). His first book sets that conviction to work, by stimulating those experiencing the text to enter fully into the spirit of its playful activity, to actualize the power and realize for themselves the felicity that instability confers, by writing their own *Nature* from scratch. The ideal philosophy founded on experience, a building of certitude on doubt, stability on flux, thus opens the way to the most irrefragable of integrations. If "perception makes" (*JMN* 13:51)—Emerson's adaptation of Berkeley's *esse est percipi*—the prospect of reconciling all differences, as between man and nature, reader and text, cannot help but be assured of realization—in each solitary seer's mind, at least.

Montaigne had likewise meditated on the effect of seeing the shore, countryside, towns, and sky from a moving ship. All move up and down, taking their motion from the observer and his angle of vision. "Nous entrainons tout avec nous," he ends the reflection (*Essais* 2.13.269). An image of himself, "le monde n'est qu'une branloire perenne" (3.2.20), a pendulum swinging to and fro in rhythm (how could it be otherwise?) with the imagination that impels it. The mind's eye gives the world a pictorial air, as Salvador Dali's illustration for "Of the Force of the Imagination" helps the reader of Cotton's translation to visualize: the artist pictures boulders, stone blocks, trees, buildings, and people rising into the air.[42] In Montaigne as in Emerson, such optical trickery testifies to a radical identity of mind and world by displaying the imagination's powers of metamorphosis. The skeptic's exercises in relativity illustrate that the observer and what he sees are as inseparable as up and down, one being the reversed or inverted mirror image of the other; and that only when taken together do they constitute the reality of the whole. "Les contraires se rejoignent [dans les *Essais*]," as Jean Rousset summarizes Montaigne's seminal contribution to the baroque themes of *trompe l'oeil* and metamorphosis.[43] Emerson concurs: "Montaigne said, himself was all he knew," and what he knew was of a piece: "as self means Devil so it means God" (*JMN* 4:68). In a journal entry of 1836 that proposes a view inviting comparison with Heraclitus's—"The way up and down is one and the same," reckons Montaigne's "le Ténebreux" (2.9.74)[44]—he repeats this conviction of the character's underlying integrity: "Read it forward or backward . . . it still spells the same thing" (*JMN* 5:184). The spectacle of the world, "a palace whose walls are lined with mirrors" (*JMN* 8:16), necessarily spells the same identity. Seen during a "dreamlike travelling on a railroad," a "Hell in harness" able to go "back or forward with equal celerity," the visible universe perplexes by its ambiguity. Which does it show at work, "the devil or the seraphim" (*JMN* 8:335, 4:296, 10:25)? So much is nature a unity that, like the character that sets the world dancing, it is impenetrable to the light of distinction-loving reason.

But if one cannot clearly distinguish the heavenly from the infernal in the nature of men and things, one can distinctly locate the provenance of that ambiguity in terms of values embraced. Montaigne, with an equanimity that the Emersonian agent of unitary reality will come to know, writes this of his allegiance(s): "À la verité . . . je porterois facilement au besoin une chandelle à S. Michel, l'autre à son serpent" (3.1.7), to which André Gide's wry humor approvingly responds, "Voici qui peut, à coup sûr, plaire plus au serpent qu'à Saint-Michel."[45] An "assistant" to Emerson's idealism (and, coincidentally, another of Gide's favorite artists) confirms that identification of the self-reliant mind's party of preference: Heaven is Hell, Hell Heaven, but only "When view'd from Hell's gate," according to Blake's "Upside-Down" reading of Dante.[46] By the logic of topsy-turvydom, it follows, the Angel of Discord can, in accordance with his own doctrine and in his own despite, be brought to plead the cause of a blessed reconciliation and so serve as an agent of a divine comedy.

Not surprisingly, it is the medieval *Divine Comedy,* set standing on its head in Blake-like fashion, that comes to serve as the primary source of Emersonian tropes for the much sought-after principle of unity implicitly contained in the doctrine taught by Milton's Satan and seconded by Montaigne's skepticism, of the mind's power to play with the universe as with a bauble. A bitterly cold day of November 1848 brings this reflection, for example: "'Tis a pretty revolution which is effected in the landscape by simply turning your head upside down, or looking through your legs. . . . It changes the landscape from November to June. . . . Massachusetts is Italy upside down" (*JMN* 10:56).[47] Idealism's antic playing makes cold hot, hot cold. Dante's *Inferno,* certainly fresh in Emerson's mind from the page proofs of Dr. John Carlyle's translation (he had carried these with him on the *Europa* only a few months before), pictures a similar "pretty revolution." At the innermost frozen circle of Hell, where its regent initially suggests a turning windmill to the pilgrim's eyes tricked by lurid light, some shades lie on their backs, some stand erect, others on their heads, while one looks like a bow, his face bent to his feet (*Inferno* 34.4, 13–15). There, as *Paradise Lost* translates the medieval oxymoron resuming Hell's grammar, "cold performs th'effect of fire" (2.295). The principle of reconciliation is close at hand. "Extremes meet," Coleridge finds illustrated in that line,[48] which aphorism Emerson extends so as to emphasize the inherent circularity of the logic it renders: "Extremes meet: there is no straight line" (*JMN* 8:397).[49]

Given this fundamental principle, there is poetic justice in the choice of an unfallen archangel, Uriel, ruler of "th'arch-chemic sun" in *Paradise Lost* (3.609), to state the case for unreason's universal dominion in the Emerson poem of 1839 bearing his name:[50]

> "Line in nature is not found;
> Unit and universe are round;
> In vain produced, all rays return;
> Evil will bless, and ice will burn."
>
> (*W* 9:14)

Uriel's cosmology asserts Hell's wholeness. On that teaching, with its emphasis on the felicitous vanity of understanding's light, Emerson builds his vision of what it is to be happy and sound. As the 1844 essay "Nature" exclaims of the enchanting spectacle of the world, an image of the wondrous whole which is character, "It is cold flame; what health, what affinity!" (*W* 3:171). "I think if I were professor of Rhetoric . . . I should use Dante for my text-book," Emerson thought to himself in 1849 (*JMN* 11:133). He actually needed no formal appointment to do so.

The poet, the "divine physician" (*JMN* 13:238–39), most fully exemplifies for Emerson the curative power of the logic figured in Dante's underworld. "A true logician," according to "Poetry and Imagination" (*W* 8:39), this most resolute of idealists unmakes differences and unites opposites by the dream-power which night makes available to all. His is the "double consciousness" of the dreamer, "at once *sub* and *objective*," making an "identity" of the pursuer and pursued, the striker and the struck, in the formulation of Emerson's "Demonology" (*EL* 3:155). *Dumque petit, petitur*—while he pursues he is pursued—as Montaigne had copied from Ovid's account of the lover enchanted with his own image in water (*Metamorphoses* 3.44; *Essais* 2.12.259). Division is an impossible as unrequited love in that ideal state of affairs. The poet is *Volvox globator* in the pink, the lover and beloved, the finished soul, the reader reading himself: Narcissus, Hermaphroditus, and Ouroboros or "the snake with its tail in the mouth" (*W* 9:140; *JMN* 11:417, 230, 8:380, 246).[51] He is the complete man, self-contained and spherical, whose *"gai science,"* the "science of love," rounds all the universe into a unity (W 8:37; JMN 9:442). Self-poised as he is in his dreamy world of ideas—they are "the daemonical band which hoops in and reconciles the contradiction of Unity & Alterity" (JMN 9:330)—[52] the poet can justly claim that he sees and knows all. Differences of all kinds melt away by virtue of that omniscience: "the All seen cures" (JMN 12:341).

So integral is the universe of the poet's ideal vision that the distance between heaven and hell is not to be measured there. His "holy glee" as he detects in his dreaming "the ultimate oneness of the Seer & the spectacle" (JMN 8:70) is the very joy of heaven, that realm of pure mind which Emerson imagines in the heady "Celestial Love,"

> Where the starred eternal worm
> Girds the world with bound and term;
> Where unlike things are like;
> Where good and ill,
> And joy and moan,
> Melt into one.
>
> (W 9:115)

The poet ministers in just such a way to a humanity sick with discord. A turning of hell's roundabout logic against itself, his synthetic art provides a mirror in which to read the way to health and joy. "He turns the woe of Night, / By its own craft, to a more rich delight," Emerson's "Bacchus" sings in celebration of the poet's logic, his composing of unity from spin (W 9:125). In the words of Nietzsche's "The Intoxicated Song," which owes much of its dizzying night-thinking to Emerson, that state of delight is a "divine hell."[53] It is, according to Howard Nemerov's more recent corroboration in "Glass Dialectic," the happy state of the model dreamer Narcissus: "From very hell your eyes reverse the world," the poet simultaneously addresses the reader reading himself and the mythic lover identical with the object of his desire.[54] Using "bitumen, fastest of cements," drawn from "the floor of the Pit," in the language of Emerson's "Uses of Great Men," this most completely realized of humanity's leading exemplars, the poet, makes "all things cohere" (W 4:24, 17). The Emersonian poet's creation, its infernal syntax pictured live in the delightful circling of Narcissus, represents idealism's highest refinement in the art of metaphysical healing.

Emerson's view of the poet's ministry coincides precisely with the ideal conception he has of his own work as healer and educator. A publicizing of "man-thinking" in strict soliloquy, his own poetic prose scribes circles true to the all-encompassing law that teaches flames to freeze and ice to boil: in act as in statement, he shows himself a faithful "Inamorato of laws, & new Narcissus" (*JMN* 11:108). And his enterprise meets with a fitting success. Since, as he lectures, "the great object of education" is "to teach self-trust" or "the absolute self-sufficiency of the mind" (*EL* 2:199, 146), the opacity that comes of solipsism and roundabout thinking has great pedagogical or medicinal virtue. With justification, defenses of Emerson's efficacy as a moral leader repeatedly come to rest on that point, stressing the power of his mystifying locutions to drive the reader back on his own devices. Elizabeth Palmer Peabody's "Nature—A Prose Poem" (1838), for example, responds to readers who look to Emerson's first book for guidance but find only a darkness of unintelligibilities, that they simply do not appreciate the author's purpose: he offers "nothing in the way of solution, so that nothing can be darkly said."[55] *Nature* is a lyric poem, all private, all process. According to George Santayana's suggestion a half century later, Emerson's is perhaps a "fortunate incapacity" to articulate clearly and explicitly. A philosopher with a more lucid understanding would have tended to intrude on the privacy and therefore the freedom of others.[56] For Lewis Leary in 1980, Emerson shows man-thinking at his best when he shows him at one with himself: "His best books are circular, their ends curving back to their beginnings." Self-enclosed as they are, their domain is "private, not public policy."[57] Opaque to the public understanding, Emerson's best books show him, in his own words, "a reading man," "self-entertained" and self-instructed, like "the serpent with its tail in the mouth" (*JMN* 8:246).

It would seem, then, that the best educator in the Emersonian scheme of things is the man who "leads out" not at all. The divinely self-sphered teacher "giving birth to himself out of the womb of his own fertile imagination," according to the diagnosis of Joel Porte's *Representative Man: Ralph Waldo Emerson in His Time* (1979),[58] would compel his uncomprehending students to do the same, to look into the mirror of those published dreams his imagination has generated and write their own divine comedies. Like the perhaps "halfwitted boy" Emerson imagined meeting on Allhallows' Eve, 1848, the true leader's name is "new Narcissus" and his judgment "infallible" (*JMN* 11:39). He teaches from omniscience, and what he says is gospel: every man for himself, each pilgrim his own Dante and Virgil, to each reader his own heaven.

The infallibility of the new Narcissus is a bracing certitude. Kin to the satanic rhetorician modeled in *Society and Solitude*, "he cannot be defeated or put down" (*W* 7:97), since logical argument and material evidence carry no weight in the autogeneal dreamer's world. "If whatever we say is irrational," as Stanley Rosen's *Nihilism: A Philosophical Essay* (1969) mimics the argument of radical subjectivity, "then certainly we can say anything we like, including that we alone are rational."[59] Narcissus does, however, exact a heavy price from the educator or reader who takes him for a patron. "Idealism . . . can never be got the better of" (*JMN* 3:71), it is certain. But, just as certainly, to use a proverb close to the heart of Emerson, the Devil will have his due.

At what price absolute autonomy Emerson spells out in an evocation of the kitten famous for having played with Montaigne:

> Do you see that kitten chasing so prettily her own tail. If you could see with her eyes you would see her surrounded with hundreds of figures performing complex dramas, with tragic & comic issues . . . many ups & downs of fate, & meantime it is only puss & her own tail. How long before . . . we shall suddenly find it was all a solitary performance. (*JMN* 8:259)[60]

The self-important kitten's playing with herself is a triviality, strictly private business and only amusing. She is like the Plato of *Representative Men* and the *Essais*. "Self-poised and spherical" as she is in the Platonic way, her whirling motion figures the dream-philosopher's circular logic: he says "one thing in one place, and the reverse of it in another," according to "Plato; or, the Philosopher" (*W* 4:55, 76). He is an artist, "great . . . by synthesis," a nimble performer delightful to watch in his endless game of flipping coins, seeing both sides of the medal (*W* 4:55). Montaigne had reckoned not so very differently. The man able to blow both hot and cold ("de mesme bouche souffler le chaud et le froid") cannot mean to be taken seriously; and Plato is such a one (1.32.266, 2.12.177). The sight of the representative thinker in action is as fit to provoke laughter as the spectacle of kitty's all-encompassing self-pursuit. Regrettably, however, as Montaigne's Diogenes jokes to himself and his bemused spectators once he has done masturbating in full view, performances of the self-enclosed kind are, for all practical purposes, empty and sterile. The self-centered man is well able to please himself and bring smiles to his audience, but rub his stomach as he will, he cannot feed himself (2.12.250). Ideal roasts are cheap, but not very filling (3.5.95).

Emerson sometimes shares that regret. When told by a sculptor that his contemplations are only "the masturbation of the brain," for example, he records the remark in his journal without comment (*JMN* 13:84). The tacit assent that his silence implies is confirmed by Emerson's own estimate when he confesses to himself: "I am wholly private: such is the poverty of my constitution" (*JMN* 16:275).

Narcissism beggars the educator and his work, making "two precious madmen" of himself and his reader, the tutor and his pupil (*JMN* 9:244). Each is self-feeding, absolutely self-reliant, and cannot possibly, except in a negative way, have anything to impart to anyone else. Nor should they want or need to, since each is already whole and infallible in his solitary performance. The cost to learning is proportionate to that solitude, and it is substantial: "At the end of these fine streets is the Lunatic Asylum" (*JMN* 11:15)—or the mental poorhouse. So teaches the teacher, that teaching is for naught; so studies the student, that study is for naught. The joke is divine, though not always altogether delightful to see. The sight of the play of self-contradiction in the new Narcissus can be pretty grim at times:

> The hero is not fed on sweets,
> Daily his own heart he eats.
>
> (W 2:249)

He regales himself as only the completely self-sufficient can.

And yet, the horrific difficulties that "solipsistic entrapment"[61] presents seem not insuperable for Emerson. Everything must come round, even the Devil's doctrine. "There is much to say on all sides," as Emerson sees reflected in Montaigne "the Proteus," who neither affirms nor denies propositions, but, like Plato, says one thing in one place and the reverse of it in another (W 4:156–57). Free to take any position at will and unconstrained by the principle of noncontradiction, the skeptic and the philosopher can be all things to all men. They can no more be identified or penned in than can the author of *Representative Men*, who reads his own logic and protean shape-shifting in the mirror of theirs. Himself a "circular philosopher . . . arrived at a fine Pyrrhonism"—the epithet of his self-apostrophe in "Circles" (W 2:317)—Emerson has no difficulty reversing direction and denying in one place the dogma of the self-sufficient and synthetic mind he elsewhere affirms. In principle, there is nothing to prevent him from taking on the guise of the realist (in contradistinction to the idealist as subjectivist) and breaking out of the solitary's madhouse.

Here he is, *à rebours*, backing away from the asylum of the all-compassing mind:

> [T]he existing world is not a dream. (W 1:303)

> "The Eternal hath fixed his canon 'gainst self slaughter" shall be my answer to the Pyrrhonist. (*JMN* 3:173)

We should not fabricate a heaven in our heads & then square life to that fiction. (*JMN* 4:42)

And do you think the painter cares to be the subject which he paints? [. . .] There are steps & limitations in the Universe, & not a huddle of identity only. (*JMN* 9:195)

Virtues speak to virtues, vices to vices—each to his own kind. (*W* 8:92)

[Ignoring differences] is joining together what God has put asunder (*JMN* 2:250).

Marriage . . . is impossible because of the inequality between every subject and every object. (*W* 3:77)

The mind does not create what it perceives, any more than the eye creates the rose. (*W* 4:82)

"The come-and-go of the pendulum, is the law of the mind," as Emerson lectures in "Resources," printed in *Letters and Social Aims* (*W* 8:150). Counterswinging to the position of the realist, who argues that objects are distinct from each other and exist in themselves apart from the mind's consciousness, this Emerson jocularly twits himself for his absurdity in trying to mesmerize himself, to spin his own top (*JMN* 10:163); affirms that external points of reference are essential to successful navigation on all seas (*W* 7:34); finds "hateful" the "private judgment" that brings "individual doctrinaires & schismatics," making of every man "a church apiece" (*JMN* 10:177–78); and avers that what the mind pines for is a good other than merely itself: "There is in the mind a subjective or inward sense of stability, which demands some outward or objective type of the same" (*EL* 3:26). "The starved camel lives on his humps" (*JMN* 14:325), but even for this he must first have found water elsewhere to drink. Of the well-watered camel there is no need to speak.

Thus Emerson breaks the fatal circle of absolute self-sufficiency and in the guise of realism's advocate eludes the mind's self-entrapment. But he does so, comically enough, by a turnabout of self-contradiction *à coup sûr* more pleasing to his representative philosopher Plato and the prince of egotists Montaigne than to the mentor of realists, Aristotle. The sickness of a "suicidally selfish, all illogical world" (*JMN* 8:137) is happily cured by suicidal unreason. To adapt one of Emerson's own borrowed maxims, the illness serves as its own antidote. True to the Devil's doctrine, he denies it.

By Emerson's calculation, however, the cure which opens a door to the outside world comes at a price easily as great as that of solipsism. A diriment impediment to the consummation of divine unions on earth, realism beggars the dreamer. If subject and object are not actually identical, the claim for introspection's power to rid the world of all differences is fatally flawed. The logical price is very high for the author of *Nature,* and therefore one reluctantly to be paid. It is a measure of the attraction the new Narcissus holds for Emerson that, even when counterworking in the realist's cause, he does not quite recant the dreamer's creed; he perseveres in claiming omnipotence for the poet, even as he checks himself with assertions of the mind's powerful limitations. "More practical and concrete" though he may appear to become in time, with such works as *English Traits* (1856) and *The Conduct of Life* (1860), he does not abandon the "old mysticism" of the 1830s.[62] Emerson's enthusiasm for poetic genius as "a sort of stoical Plenum nullifying the Comparative" (*JMN* 7:36) proves resistant and retains the power to inspire followers. According to Sanford E. Marovitz's celebration in 1982, for example, the Emerson of *Parnassus,* published nearly four decades after *Nature,* continues to "transubstantiate" what he reads: "In 'the supreme genius' of Shakespeare, truth and beauty, spirit and nature, fused, as seeming contraries merged in Emerson himself and became one."[63] The distinction between this Emerson, his Shakespeare of 1874, and the incarnated Omnipotent is hardly to be divined. The world, it would seem, still moves at the poet's beckoning.

Another, less obvious, indication of Emerson's reluctance to part with the dreamer at one with his universe is the absence of Narcissus by name from speculations focusing on the poet's (and his own) inability or failure to unify himself with the objective world. Perhaps the analogy between this shortcoming and that of the ancient Narcissus impossibly pining to be wed to another is so transparent that Emerson feels no need to spell it out. Read more comprehensively, however, in the light of Emersonian thinking generally, the discreet neglect suggests a subtle stratagem to spare the new Narcissus the fate of the old. In those instances where Emerson shifts into the realist's mode and deems futile the attempt to identify mind and matter, sign and signified, the figure made to convey the burden of limitation is not Narcissus at all, old or new, but Tantalus. Analogical substitution follows mythical displacement, with the apparent effect of further distancing radical idealism from its consequences. It is no solipsist, but an underworld figure only too much aware of the mind's inability to feed itself, who simultaneously suffers the Ovidian dreamer's futility in his stead and spares Emerson's representative mythical idealist, whether as Satan or Narcissus, from the agonizing role as model for the poet of diminished power. The play of misdirection and substitution is well designed to draw attention away from the perils of self-sufficiency. Meanwhile, in terms of rhetorical effect at least, the delightful new Narcissus is left alone, to dream his dream in undisturbed peace. The futility of Tantalus's endless reaching seems not to touch the pursuer pursued: "Of course, these & no others, interest us; these dear & beautiful beings who are absorbed in their own dream" (*JMN* 10:339).

But the undertone of wistfulness in Emerson's voice when it speaks in this way is as eloquent as his silent disjunction of Narcissus from his fate. It speaks of a loss. Though reluctantly at bottom, Emerson does not abandon the mirror logic of his circular philosophy when it calls for a denial of the dreamer's power to compass all differences. *Alii disputent; ego mirabor,*" his self-perception in a letter of March 1838 (*L* 2:123), precisely summarizes the turn of mind that permits him to unsay his doctrines of identity and the mind's beatific self-reliance. If the mind, like the eye that commands the world from a moving coach, is the idealist's abode of divine unity, a reversed perspective instantly converts it to the place of Tantalus, Emerson the realist's emblem for a humanity fallen short of the absolute: "What a Tantalus cup this life is! The beauty that shimmers on these yellow afternoons who ever could clutch it? Go forth and find it, & it is gone; 'tis only a mirage as you look from the windows of a diligence" (*JMN* 5:97). Man craves substantial nourishment, but drinks only from a cup filled with illusions of his own making. Like the Narcissus of ancient fable, Emerson's Tantalus-man cannot possibly reach out and clutch an other that is truly other than himself. He is damned to everlasting fruitless inanition. Man so conceived can no more realize "the vision of the perfect . . . than he can set foot on the horizon which flies before him" (*EL* 3:13). The perfection of Emerson's divinely spherical new Narcissus now becomes the futility of his tortured Tantalus. True to his creed, he turns the tables on himself, comes full circle, and makes a hell of his heaven.

Understandably, it is the most fully representative of men, the poet, who suffers most in the transposition, by inversion, to a world of objective objects. Since the seer and the seen are no longer the same there, "the poet finds himself not near enough to his object" (*W* 3:190). His aim, "the conquest of the Universe," is consequently "impracticable" (*JMN* 10:162), and his vision of a beatific unity on earth a chimera. What is needed is "a good cook, a good gizzard, that can digest religions, railroads, revolutions & make poetry of them all," Emerson declared in 1848 (*JMN* 11:46). But the poet has his limitations, and what synthesis his digestion is able to produce proves unsatisfying fare in the end. The poet can no more mend all differences by dreaming than a blinded shepherd lost in a snowstorm—"an emblem of the state of man"—can find his way home by groping (W 3:33). The objective eludes his grasp. If art, like life, is a self-enclosed dream, as Emerson frequently reread in Montaigne's "Des coches" ("Of Coaches," by Cotton's simplification), the artist going abroad in search of food for the mind does no more than travel in circles: "Nous nous promenons sur nos pas" (3.6.122). So poignant and palpable is the vanity of such an enterprise that, *à contrecoeur*, in a way familiar to Emerson, Montaigne is driven to concur with Cicero's *De finibus*—*nulla ars in se versatur* (3.6.118)—even as his own inconclusive art, "un serpent qui se mord la queue,"[64] advances the contrary, that all art *is* self-enclosed. For Emerson as well, traveling in search of external sustenance is "ridiculous": "the world is a treadmill," and the quester's sense of actually moving toward a goal nothing more than a trick of the eye (*JMN* 7:220). Try as the self-reliant man will, as Emerson figures him in "The Poet" (1844), he falls short of his goal and dies within a few feet of his door (W 3:33). The "world of approximations," of similitudes only and not identities, is "all tantalizing" (*JMN* 12:458), and its inhabitants starve for want of true nourishment. How, then, is Emerson to make good his cherished optimism against this hell? The case would seem hopeless.

"Now that the age of reflection is arrived shall we not eat its good fruit?" Emerson asks, inviting his public to dine in a lecture of 1836 (*EL* 2:20). The affirmation that "Tantalus is but the name for you and me" (W 2:32) suggests this translation: Now that the age of reflection has arrived shall we not eat its bitter fruit of inanition and futility? Emerson is ironically warning his audience against the vanity of the age and its impending results. But this would be to read him as though his valuations were closer to Dante's than to Montaigne's. The cat of the woodcuts gracing the 1578 Venice edition of the *Divine Comedy*, unlike the kitten Emerson borrows from the *Essais*, has its eyes fixed on food other than itself; and, unlike the figure of starvation in Hades, comes to a satisfying conclusion: as pictured after the last line of the *Paradiso*, the cat has obviously come to eat its fill.[65] Matters rest otherwise with Emerson, who again inverts the medieval comedy: "happy the soul which is . . . dissatisfied" (*L* 5:428). If the new Narcissus knows the beatitude of perfect coincidence, Tantalus knows the beatitude of imperfect approximation. In the Emersonian world, where "every truth is a full circle" (*JMN* 4:381), it is possible to have one's cake and eat it too.

The indigence Tantalus suffers is precious to Emerson. "We must hold hard to this poverty," he insists in "Experience" (1844) (W

3:81). The differences that impoverish by making impossible the complete union of seer and seen, reader and text, nature and mind, are a measure of man's divineness, "the infinitude of the private man" (*JMN* 7:342). "All barriers . . . only whet the thirst" (*JMN* 14:17): the more the bootless reaching after wholeness, the more the craving for it; the more the craving, the more the reaching. The vicious circling of "remediless thirst" (*JMN* 9:26) has great virtue in Emerson's eyes, for it guarantees man's immortality, his inconclusiveness, however tormenting. The fact that "one is led forever on, in an endless Circle" (*JMN* 14:141) gives Emerson and his archangel Uriel just cause for jubilation: "O endless ends" (*JMN* 11:181). Though at the opposite pole from the plenum of indifference proclaimed by Milton's Satan and lived by the new Narcissus, the Hades of Tantalus is no less divinely blissful in its torment. The very emptiness of Tantalus, "the great deep [which] . . . is Eternal Man" (*JMN* 8:24), answers to the Infinite, conceived not as Plenitude itself, but its opposite, "the Immeasurable unimaginable pit of Emptiness" (*JMN* 8:67). "Deep calls unto deep," according to Emerson's gospel in the final chapter of *Nature*, where he immediately goes on to add, with regret: "But in actual life, the marriage is not celebrated" (*W* 1:74). Emerson is not so glum. In the ideal world of his thought, where extremes meet and the infinite deep of hell calls unto the infinite deep of heaven, the marriage is celebrated with gusto. His imagination sees all and he rejoices; his imagination sees nothing and he rejoices. Emerson the ambidextrous proves himself right: the man faithful to the fallen Lucifer's way of thinking is always hard to keep down.

In 1823, some two years after his graduation from Harvard College, Emerson resolved "to make closer acquaintance with the world within." He would "extinguish the Sun" and "annihilate this solid fabric of earth" (*JMN* 2:130). How resolutely he kept to that promise his subsequent works show. Endlessly circling in the underworld within, Emerson's night-thinking effectively puts out the light of understanding in himself, and serves him well in his vocation as moral educator. Darkness calls unto darkness; and the reader, reaching out to grasp some affirmation in Emerson, only to see it disappear on being approached, converted to its opposite,[66] is tutored in the vanity of enlightenment. Like the capricious Montaigne, the mercurial Carlyle, and the Boston pilot stripped of his certificate of competence in 1848, Emerson is a nimble shifter. Such tantalizing is fitted to delight not only the teacher who teaches that teaching is for naught, but also the student prizing logic and learning: a tutor exalting ignorance cannot mean to be taken too seriously. And so, their relationship is mutually pleasing, though in opposite ways. The (un)teacher is successful in teaching nothing and the student who takes learning seriously is made merry.

As the response of the ship's master who once tried to teach Emerson how to get a fix on his position in sunshine serves to illustrate, ignorance can be a joking matter and experts in unknowing sprightly entertainers: "The good Captain rejoices much in my ignorance" (*JMN* 4:111). Certainly, the notion that "the fable of the Wandering Jew is agreeable to men" because it speaks to the pleasure humanity takes in the idea of infinity (*W* 8:338–39), of "endless embarcations entered inward," on the "unharboured Deep" (*JMN* 8:294, 4:65), must strike the mind that values direction and conclusion as inherently comical. Unlike the Wandering Jew of Coleridge's *Rime of the Ancient Mariner*, whose tale leaves its listener a sadder and a wiser man, Emerson's tells a fable to delight. The legend of the *Flying Dutchman*, a wonderworking vessel condemned forever to round the Cape of Good Hope, presumably speaks of the felicity of inconclusiveness in a similarly agreeable way. So manifestly playful are Emerson's topsy-turvy antics that they cannot horrify. Rather, they are acts of self-disqualification from the responsibility of the navigator, making of Emerson a harmless comic. Not for him the serious work of a divine comedian with eyes turned outward and upward. He is only a diverting landlubber, a man of infinite jest.

3
Melville's Mute Glass

Je m'aide à perdre ce que je serre particulierement.
—Montaigne, "De la praesumption"

... an enigma before you—smiling, frowning, inviting, grand, mean, insipid, or savage, and always mute with an air of whispering, Come and find out.
—Conrad, *Heart of Darkness*

IN October 1885, a month or so before resigning his nineteen-year post as a respected and trusted customs inspector in New York, Herman Melville sent Mrs. Ellen Marett Gifford his new photograph. While the face imaged is "the veritable face (at least, so says the Sun that never lied in his life)," he observes in the genially ironic accompanying letter, its "so serious" look belies the "frolicsome" self he recalls from a little rhyme of his about Montaigne and his cat. Melville playfully extends this invitation: "Pray, explain the inconsistency, or I shall begin to suspect your venerable friend of being a two-faced old fellow and not to be trusted."[1] *Que sçais-je?* the letter muses with the skeptic, and gives no answer. *The Confidence-Man: His Masquerade,* which marks the end of Melville's career as a public writer of fiction in 1857, also queries the trust one can place in uncertain reflections. On the face of it, Melville proffers no answer there either. He has "no settled voice . . . forever trying on alternatives," vacillating, it is generally remarked, in "a dialectic or continuing dialogue between the Yea-sayers and the Nay-sayers."[2] The various, often contradictory, readings the work has invited stand as confirmation of such an alleged lack of resolution.[3]

But a settled answer is available in *The Confidence-Man,* providing access to the end and ending of that fiction and the silence that consequently follows it. *The Confidence-Man* marks the term of Melville's developing sense of "the Truth" and "the great Art of

Telling" it,[4] an action in contraries. "Unlike things must meet and mate: / A flame to melt—a wind to freeze," as he wrote in "Art,"[5] one of the *Timoleon* poems privately printed in the year of his death, 1891. The answer proposed is this: that, being paradoxical, wisdom or understanding and the expression of that wisdom are vain. The oppositions active in wisdom and art come to cancel themselves out for Melville, who logically concludes in silence. In the words of *Religio Medici's* adaptation of Florio's Montaigne, "contraries . . . destroy one another" even as they are "the life of one another."[6]

Pray, explain the inconsistency.

A grimly playful double-dealing harlequin had similarly asked for enlightenment some thirty years before, in the final chapter of that riddling symposium on faith and truth, faces and counterfeits, *The Confidence-Man*. How can that be trustworthy that teaches distrust?" Frank Goodman asks of an old reader of the Bible. They are discussing "the Wisdom of Jesus, the Son of Sirach," in particular the maxim "Take heed of thy friends" (6:13).[7] The scene, it will be remembered, locates the discussion in a circle of light scribed by a solar lamp, "the light of the Old and New Testaments,"[8] with sleepers, unquiet or content, in a gradually diminishing illumination on the periphery. "How can that be trustworthy that teaches distrust?"—the question's syntax suggests that Sirach's wisdom is "apocryphal" not merely because uncanonical (for Protestants, at least); it is "something of uncertain credit" by reason of paradox (208–9). "Look on all the works of the Most High; they are always in pairs, one the opposite of the other," pronounces the Book of Sirach (33:15). Though the Old Testament author is located "right in the middle of this enormous tension,' as Gerhard von Rad comments in *Wisdom in Isreal* (1970), his teaching is "neither gloomy nor tormented; it is, rather, underpinned by a great confidence."[9] In the eyes of the author of *The Confidence-Man*, however, who could "neither believe, nor be comfortable in his unbelief," according to Hawthorne's reckoning in November 1856 (*ML* 2:529), the presence of contradiction subverts confidence: the sage asks for trust even as he warns against it, undermining the reader's faith in what he says. As Goodman reads further from the Book of Sirach, the reader of *The Confidence-Man* is encouraged to extend such a line of reasoning to the whole enterprise of wisdom trafficking.

"What is seen in dreams is to reality what the reflection of a face is to the face itself," writes Sirach (34:3), who confidently identifies the fool with the dreamer and ironically confirms himself as a fool and a dreamer when he goes on to record, "all we see is but a flash"

(42:23). "Like the wheel of a cart is the mind of a fool; his thoughts revolve in circles," he warns (33:5), seemingly coiled in self-reflection. Read in this way, with the ironic vision Melville himself found as the defining feature of an "atheistical" Renaissance commentator on "sacred matters" in October 1856 (*ML* 2:523), the apocryphal words, "Take heed of thy friends," mirror the canonical precepts of charity from 1 Corinthians (13:4–8) copied out for the *Fidèle*'s passengers by the deaf-mute eventually dozing off in the first chapter of the novel. They confirm, by contradiction and similitude, the equivocal status of St. Paul's text, as lie or truth told by a sage or fool, for, immediately following "Charity believeth all things" (13:8), its author affirms that "we now know in part" only—we see not "face to face" but "through a glass darkly" (13:12).[10] Sirach's analogy of face and reflection would make of St. Paul a fellow dreamer. Since truth itself cannot be seen—so his chain of inference binds the skeptic—the wisdom reflected in words cannot avoid duplicity, speaking as it does in counterfeit and self-contradiction. The quest for understanding is consequently perilous and perplexing. "Dont be after burning your fingers with the likes of wisdom," cautions one of the slumberers interrupting Goodman and the old student of the Bible (209). *Caveat auctor, caveat lector.* As Sebastian Brant had warned in *The Ship of Fools*, "Trust not a man in any wise, / The world is false and full of lies."[11] Reader and author are set on a roundabout in obscurity.

By logic, it would seem, there can be no end in sight for the Melvillean reader after wisdom. The way of understanding is as endless as the ancient "Liar" paradox assiduously exploited by Montaigne and other Renaissance *fols sages* well known to Melville. "Can the liar ever speak the truth?" *The Confidence-Man* asks with Sirach (34:4). "Does the man who says that he is now lying, speak truly?" Eubulides of Miletus had wondered to Aristotle.[12] That conundrum, as Rosalie L. Colie's *Paradoxia Epidemica* (1966) shows, provided the syntactical model for Renaissance *insolubilia* serving to advance the claim of "ignorance" as "the true wisdom," an argument frequently sustained, as in Brant, Nicholas of Cusa, and Erasmus, by evidence from the Old Testament wisdom books and the Pauline epistles, Ecclesiastes and 1 Corinthians in particular.[13] Less the reason, less the knowledge, more the faith *or* doubt. Sir Thomas Browne, Melville's "crack'd Archangel" (*ML* 1:273), is exemplary in this regard: while he believes it is "no vulgar part of Faith to believe a thing not only above but also contrary to Reason," he is also persuaded that "the wisest heads prove, at last, almost all Scepticks, and stand like Janus in the field of knowledge."[14] *The Confidence-Man* is the work of just such a figure. It is not that the fiction "finally reduces all . . . logical considerations to complete irrelevance"—[15] without logic there is neither paradox nor absurdity—or that it adapts from *The Anatomy of Melancholy* the practice of "juxtaposing . . . contradictory Biblical passages" so as to demonstrate that "all religions" are merely "fictitious."[16] Rather, *The Confidence-Man* equivocates as paradox, read in Renaissance fashion, equivocates: "It lies, and it doesn't. It tells the truth, and it doesn't."[17] "Look a lie and find the truth," the young purveyor of patently useless counterfeit detectors ponders in the final chapter (212). As one commentator observes, "so tight is Melville's logic that even the reverse of [a] . . . paradox is true."[18] Similarly, according to a recent study of Melville's humor, to read *The Confidence-Man* is to learn "the slow necessity to read everything . . . in reverse."[19] Leading in circles, reading in this way is necessarily inconclusive.

But is nothing at all concluded in *The Confidence-Man?* The syntax of Renaissance wisdom is again instructive. If the action of paradox is infinitely reflexive, it is also "self-canceling," explains Colie, who reads that double effect in the Renaissance emblem of the Ouroboros. The snaky circle figures at once an endless revolution of opposites and their mutual cancellation: infinity and zero.[20] Like the Ouroboros—"the novel's final sentence . . . leads circularly back to the beginning"—[21] *The Confidence-Man* perpetually turns in on itself. And, like the snake with its tail in its mouth, it ends in negation. Frank Goodman finally extinguishes the lamp of wisdom and Melville concludes: "Something further may follow of this Masquerade." What follows is silence. Such a coincidence of endings implies that interpretation of the fundamental sense or end of *The Confidence-Man* can profitably seek illumination in the progress of Melville's pursuit of truth as recorded in his first novel, *Typee* (1846), to the late summer of 1856 when he finished his somber comedy of an April Fools' Day. Though circle it must be by nature, paradox is an idea and must therefore, like a life and a book, have a beginning. In the words of Henri Bergson, a logician of the comic who comes to find the taste of laughter bitter in the end, "An idea is something that grows, buds, blossoms, and ripens from the beginning to the end of a speech."[22] Melville had recourse to a similar image in an 1851 letter to Hawthorne: confessing that he reads Solomon "more & more," seeing "deeper & deeper and unspeakable meanings," he compares the development of his literary career and the course of his moral enlightenment since 1844 to the unfolding of a "bulb." The following reading of that gradual disclosure offers a way of coming to see the "inmost leaf" or center to which it leads (*ML* 1:413).

* * *

Melville's career as published author was launched in 1846 with a plea for trust. Since his narrative tells "the unvarnished truth," he insists in the preface to *Typee,* readers must have "confidence" in it: the "facts" and "the conclusions deduced from these facts" admit of "no contradiction" (viii–ix). Some early readers took him at his word. The *Home Journal,* for example, printed a call for "an humble, unquestioning reliance on the word of the narrator," and "a literary tribunal" in the *Almanack of the Month* acquitted Melville of any forgery (*ML* 1:220). Others believed the contrary. One reader pronounced *Typee* "a piece of Munchausenism"; another called into question even the existence of one "Herman Melville" (*ML* 1:211, 224). Melville was vexed by the doubters: "The fact is, those who do not believe it are the greatest 'gulls,'" he writes in a letter of May 1846 (*ML* 1:214). So sharp was his vexation that Melville, ex-president of the Philo-Logos (Debating) Society of Albany, prepared a formal defense of *Typee* as a genuine narrative and offered the anonymous piece to a New York newspaper (*ML* 1:214). He would "stop the mouths of the senseless sceptics" such as had spoken in the *Journal des débats* (*ML* 1:226–27, 219).[23] And with a view further to encourage the reader's confidence, Melville included in the revised edition of *Typee* a brief sequel, "Story of Toby," incorporating the corroborative testimony of Richard Tobias Greene, the self-acknowledged "true and veritable 'Toby'" of the narrative (*ML* 1:220).[24]

Melville very much needed his reader's confidence, since *Typee* itself attempted to redress erroneous reading by the gulled consumers of travel books. As Melville's narrator Tommo (Tom) relates his experiences among aboriginal Marquesans, he offers a corrective to "popular fictions" about life in the South Seas (276). His account must be more believable than these, which lie by locating truth at the extremities of an antithesis. Tommo removes the veil of deception by recounting his own undeceiving from lying stories. "Typee or Happar?" is the question for the unmasking of such falsehood (87, 91, 94, 101). The Happar tribe has among whites "a reputation for gentleness and humanity"; the Typee, for savage cruelty (66–67). But as Tommo and his companion Toby discover, the Typees can in fact be cultivated and gentle. The reputation of the Happars is also shown to be unjustified in part: they almost kill Toby. Nor are the natives less prone to err than the white man. Each of the tribes creates fictions, each making itself entirely virtuous and the other entirely vicious. Happar or Typee, civilization or savagery, virtue or vice, are weak, not strong disjunctives. "Truth, who loves to be centrally located, is

". . . found between the two extremes," *Typee* concludes (227). As the facts of his experience argue, the truth resides in a mean, not in either the "cold shiverings" or the "burning fever" the beguiled Tommo suffers early in the narrative (63). But the thesis stands only if those facts are believed.

The solution of life's ambiguity in the truth of a mean, however, did not hold Melville long. In December 1846, he completed *Omoo*, which leads to no conclusive inference. While the truth claim made for this work is the same as for *Typee*—it is "a circumstantial history of adventures befalling the author," an "unbiased observer" strictly adhering to "facts" (vii–viii)—the facts now locate the narrator in a mad funhouse without exit. Escaping from what has become a prison in Eden, Tommo joins the uproariously mischievous crew of a rat-infested ship and lands in jail. Every significant action in this narrative that includes an ugly ship's carpenter named Beauty has the "contrary result" to the one anticipated by reason (19, 363). A drunken first mate without benefit of chronometer navigates brilliantly; a captain takes a seaman's pulse to determine whether he is a Sydney man or a Yankee and decides correctly; and gestures of friendship end in a macabre farce of bloodshed. *Omoo*, in fact, relates a series of jokes designed according to the recoil principle, as illustrated in the firing of a musket by Dr. Long Ghost, prankster and storyteller: the charge "went one way, and he the other." The piece "could not fail of doing execution," the narrator reflects, laughingly (260).

As the text of *Omoo* suggests, the joke goes so far as to include the very act of its telling. An eyewitness account of facts, *Omoo* recalls histories "enveloped in the profoundest obscurity" (14) and retells mariners' yarns, "stories . . . related as gospel truths, by those who declared themselves eye-witnesses" (55). Like the spiked cannons of Motoo-Ooto, these words play a joke on their user (193). If the narrator of *Omoo* cannot ascertain the precise truth of stories told to him by his fellow mariners—"I give it for what it is worth" (83)— how can the reader clearly discriminate between fact and fiction in the narrator's own witnessing? Melville merrily raises that serious question, engaging the doubts of some readers regarding the genuineness of *Typee* and anticipating skeptical responses to *Omoo*. And such responses there were to be, setting off a running joke in print. *Blackwood's Magazine* comically invented a life for the author in June 1847, describing *Omoo* as a fiction by a fiction, to which the *Daily Knickerbocker* replied in an announcement of Melville's marriage to Elizabeth K. Shaw in August: "No lady would marry an ideal person—a waif, a mere shadow" (*ML* 1:259, 256). Two months later, in a letter to his English publisher, Melville recalls his "diversion at the solemn incredulity" of the *Blackwood's* writer, and observes: "I only but begin, as it were, to feel my hand" (*ML* 1:263). The inconclusive jesting of *Omoo* and the comic responses it stimulated have invited a closer examination of the fundamental question: Can the truth be known with certainty?

The result of Melville's meditation on the question is made public some two years later, in *Mardi* (1849). As the romance testifies, he has been reading widely in the literature of skepticism and wisdom. Kant, Burton, Aristotle, Proclus, Erasmus, Browne, Porphyry, Spinoza, Pyrrho, Rabelais, Seneca, Dante, Shakespeare, Berkeley, Carlyle, and Montaigne are but some of the authors present in *Mardi*. If it is "a book of ill-digested eclecticism,"[25] it is nonetheless a thematically coherent narration of Melville's "quest for an authoritative principle," "the authority of certainty."[26] While the jesting of *Omoo* is occasionally repeated—a patient dies after a successful operation, for example, and the missiles of attackers fly back into their teeth—Melville is not content simply to transcribe life's comic absurdity. He now looks to articulate underlying truth by analyzing the logic basic to human activity, including the very search for wisdom itself. Specifically, he considers the operation of that logic in the interpretation of texts, an activity of paramount interest to a Melville struggling to make himself understood to his own readers. The analysis takes Melville into a circle of paradox, where he finds "everything uncertain" (*Mardi*, 1:125), offering no sure grounds for distinguishing verity from fiction in books, his own included.

Wisdom is paradoxical, Melville speculates in *Mardi*, because interpretation is uncertain. The truth-teller, like the oracle, speaks dark maxims and riddling parables because the text he reads, of man, the world, and God, is an enigmatic hieroglyphic. What that secret writing transmits are "vague hints" and "fleeting revealings," like images "darkly reflected . . . in glassy water" (1:177, 219, 2:25). Since the sage does not see truth itself, only its ambiguous reflections, he is bound to divine "truth . . . in lies" and to announce his sightings vaguely, by "tropes on tropes" (2:201–2). And the reader of his words has no sure way of telling whether those "images" are "genuine or spurious" (2:38). Mystery, then, makes a fool of both the man of insight and his interpreters, as Solomon and Montaigne confirm when they write that "all men are fools; and every wise man knows himself to be one" (1:53). "Full of enigmas," the teacher of truth speaks enigmatically, affirming and denying propositions at once (1:362; 2:2). "St. Paul . . . argues the doubts of Montaigne" even as he calls for faith, writes Melville (2:54); and Sir Thomas Browne explodes "Vulgar Errors" even as he heartily hugs "all the mysteries in the Pentateuch" (1:45). Their self-contradiction demonstrates "the stupidity of . . . sages" (2:41).

The cardinal trope for wisdom's paradox in *Mardi* is "an endless string of . . . lizards" fixed in a circle, "in inverted chase of their tails" (1:295). As the wise skeptic Babbalanja explains, "It is a perpetual cycling with us" (2:161).[27] It is perpetual cycling with this interpreter of the mystical ponderings of Old Bardiana because he equivocates: his "tongue is forked" (2:130). By ambiguous figures and baffling contradictions, Babbalanja struggles to articulate as precisely as he can the truth of a universe where distinctions between fiction and fact, waking and sleeping, life and death are unclear. A book of wisdom and a work of interpretation, *Mardi* itself tropes that equivocation, beginning with stories going "round and round," their "beginning and end . . . united for aye" (1:4), and ending with a pursuer pursued over "an endless sea." With each "folio . . . turned over for wisdom" (1:14), Melville finds the endless serpent of folly, and figures his discoveries in "an endless folio" of his own (1:278).

But if the serpent of paradox represents endless motion, it also figures annihilation. The "god of Suicides" in the land of Mardi is "a long anaconda-like image . . . wound round and round its own neck" (2:26–27), an emblem to recall Donne's *Biathanatos*, "a paradox about paradox" built on the theme of self-destruction.[28] Among the victims of such a logic is King Peepi: if "contrary impulses" set him spinning in "a ceaseless eddy," they also "annul" each other, leaving him permanently motionless, incapable of action (1:237–38). And an identical stasis results from the contradiction of two hieroglyphics: the meaning of one "nullifies the other" (2:224). Their interpreter is consequently paralyzed. So too with the wise man, who, like the Devil in "that infernalest of Infernos, the Inferno," is unendingly locked in an element of fire and ice (1:346). The coming together of contraries in paradox produces a devilish "silence" or "gray chaos," "the everlasting lull, introductory to a positive vacuity," as Melville parodies Carlyle (1:55, 10). Self-canceling, the skeptic's logic leaves him "wordless" or reduces his utterance to inarticulate nonsense: "Fugle-fi is its finis:—fugle-fi, fugle-fo, fugle-fugle-orum!" (2:215). David Hume had anticipated this conclusion. The thoroughgoing skeptic, he argues in *An Enquiry concerning Human Understanding*, "must acknowledge . . . that all human life must perish, were his principles universally and steadily to prevail. All discourse, all action would immediately cease, and men remain in a total lethargy. . . ."[29]

By that reckoning, the skeptic's reasoning beckons him to silence and death. "Il n'y auroit sans doubte remede que de mourir de soif et de faim," as Montaigne had joked with himself in "Comme nostre esprit s'empesche soy-mesmes" (2.14.275).[30]

Melville, however, sets aside for the moment the conclusion of the skeptic's wisdom in permanent inaction. He writes to Evert Duyckinck in April 1849: "Would that a man could do something & then say—It is finished. . . . But live & push—tho' we put one leg forward ten miles—its no reason the other must lag behind—no, *that* must again distance the other—& so we go till we get the cramp and die" (*ML* 1:296). Melville resolves to continue in the interminable pursuit after wisdom as long as time will permit. There is, as well, the skeptic's axiom of relativity yet to be dramatized. "There is nothing either good or bad, but thinking makes it so," he underscores in his copy of Shakespeare, adding the comment: "Here is forcibly shown the great Montaignism of Hamlet" (*ML* 1:291). "The world revolves upon an I," according to *Mardi* (2:279). On that principle Melville will raise *Moby-Dick*.

The immediate reception of *Mardi* analogically validated its speculation on the vagaries of interpretation. It was pronounced "hazy," "unreadable," "a 3-vol. metaphor." "How aught so luminous can be so dark," a critic wondered of the obscurity he found himself in, thus repeating the question already answered by the romance's hieroglyphic (*ML* 1:298, 295, 293). Melville responded to the irony of such impercipience with the heavy-handed ironies of *Redburn* and *White-Jacket*, completed in June and August, respectively. In the guise of factual reminiscences and historically accurate nautical lore, he dresses two fables insistent on the vagary of truth. "To tell the truth" (*Redburn*, 114, 129), "the truth was" (233), "no mistaking the fact" (265) remarks the narrator Redburn in a story of characters "lost in mazes" of "cabalistic figures," "lost . . . in conjectures," and deceived "with all manner of fables" (116, 160, 311–12). "No doubt," the mature autobiographer wryly interjects time and time again as he recalls his own once-certain faith in the veracity of texts. Redburn had once believed that the old green-morocco guidebook to Liverpool given to him by his father contained unerring knowledge. Now he believes otherwise: "Guide-books . . . are the least reliable books in all literature; and nearly all literature, in one sense, is made up of guide-books." All are questionable, except "the one Holy Guide-Book" (201). But the reader may find cause to doubt this last affirmation as well, for *Redburn*, too, is a parody of wisdom literature, teaching that truth is unknowable: "you know nothing till you know all; which is the reason we never know anything" (154). To reason in this way is finally to argue for the "creedless faith" of the "sceptic" (377). Melville understandably found the *Blackwood's* review of *Redburn* "very comical"—it treated "the thing as real" (*ML* 1:327), as a bona fide guidebook.

White-Jacket, or The World in a Man of War, like *Redburn*, rings with repeated assertions of positive conviction: "I must frankly tell a story" (19), "I will here frankly make confession" (250), "I let nothing slip, however small" (355), the author takes the reader into his confidence. He professes to tell the truth, the whole truth, and nothing but the truth. "Truth and fidelity forbid" leaving anything "undisclosed" (446). The posture is antic disguise, for *White-Jacket* is virtually stuffed with "cock-and-bull stories," "gossips," "conflicting and crazy surmisings," "fiction," "yarns and twisters," "rumours," and "fables" (121, 58, 499, 270, 399, 290, 490). The distinction between truth and fiction proffered in the book is as equivocal as the difference its author ironically proposes between history and legend in a biblical "yarn" (340). Similarly, differences between actors and characters elude authoritative definition in the world of the *Neversink*, where persons and personae interchange roles as in "a continual theatre" and where "counterlikes and dislikes . . . dovetail into each other" as in "a Chinese puzzle" (114, 204). All manner of players act out their parts in the theater of the *Neversink*, a seagoing analogue to "Shakespeare's . . . sacred text" (209). The oracle's oeuvre is a playhouse. And like that text, *White-Jacket* cannot avoid duplicity. As Melville had written earlier in 1849, "even Shakespeare, was not a frank man to the uttermost." The divine William's secretiveness was not simply a tactic or disguise to avoid detection and muzzling by the Elizabethan thought-police and the public they represented (*ML* 1:292). His "sermons-on-the-mount" (*ML* 1:288) could not be entirely frank since even he could not see truth wholly and clearly: truth reveals "herself . . . covertly and by snatches," "only by cunning glimpses" in "this world of lies," Melville will remark in "Hawthorne and His Mosses" (August 1850).[31] In the words of *Mardi*, "there is no telling all" (1:49).

As though to extend the logic of its duplicity, *White-Jacket* even belies its own insistence on the ambiguity of all texts and readings by earnestly preaching an unambiguous truth. Melville's book would expose and correct actual abuses in the U.S. Navy. As in *Typee*, Melville here required the full confidence of his reader if his work was to be efficacious for justice. And, as a condition for obtaining that confidence, he needed to persuade the public of his complete frankness. "Wherever statements are made . . . concerning the established laws and usages of the Navy," Melville insists in the preface to the first English edition (October 1849), "facts have been strictly adhered to" (v). A 1970 commentary corroborates the author's claim: *White-Jacket* is "a document of interesting and authoritative detail, valuable to students of naval history." It is primarily "a documentary," not "a novel." And yet, as the commentator also observes, the book is "pseudo-fictional" and "pseudo-realistic" as well, blending "fable and fact" and sometimes confusing "the literal record" of history. The subsequent claim for *White-Jacket* as "a Bible . . . authentic in its facts"[32] seems unwittingly to reproduce the conflict in the dual role Melville assigns to his book, as authentic chronicler and deceiving fabulist. The claim for the authoritative truth of a text that, by its very grammar of self-contradiction, makes truth doubtful must be a doubtful one. Like the characters its author sets playing on the *Neversink*, *White-Jacket* is a work of "strange contradictions" (493). The harlequin's motley is fit garb for a book acting out its part in a universe where "fire freezes" (126): *White-Jacket* is "a piece of patchwork."[33]

The harlequinade of *White-Jacket*, however, went virtually unnoticed by landsmen in Melville's day. The book was praised for its simplicity, clarity, and truthfulness. Some of the master practitioners of "the great Art of Telling the Truth," as Melville responds not long after, take delight "in hoodwinking the world."[34] Ironically enough, it is the literal-minded Rear-Admiral Thomas O. Selfridge, Sr. who seems to have read more accurately than the literati when he spied "inconsistencies" and "so much of the marvelous & absurd" in *White-Jacket* (*ML* 1:382).[35] The old salt had anticipated the claim for that text as a Melvillean bible. "Who well considers the Christian religion, would think that God meant to keep it in the dark from our understandings," Melville transcribes Saint-Évremond to the back flyleaf of the New Testament & Psalms given to him by his Aunt Jean Melvill in 1846 (*ML* 1:231).[36] The seventeenth-century admirer of Solomon and disciple of Montaigne had observed in each of these "de la contrariété dans ses discours et dans ses actions"; yet each, in his ignorance or self-contradiction, merits "le nom de sage."[37] By that same standard, the author of *White-Jacket* also merits the name. He, too, has seized "the right meaning of Montaigne" (63).

In October 1849, with the proofs of *White-Jacket* in his luggage, Melville took passage for England on the London liner *Southampton*. The voyage, as logged in his journal, parallels the comic journey in unreason and illusion imaged in those proofs.[38] Recording live an excursion into the absurd, the journal blurs the line between playing and being. Only a few days out of New York, Melville experiences firsthand the merry suicide of a madman, and encounters a victim of delirium tremens who has visions of invisible steamers. As the *Southampton* sails into the night, the author of *White-Jacket* imbibes copiously of brandy, punch, and wine, and talks of "high German metaphysics" with George J. Adler, a German-American who will be committed to an asylum in 1853. The revelry, pranks, and masquerades of the *Southampton's* passengers write a prelude to the "comical scene" of her arrival. And the high-spirited theatrics continue on land. While in London, Melville observes the "very comical" scene of a riotous beggars' feast, sees "very comical" performances at a theater, converses with a "comical librarian" who shows him Shakespeare's autograph in a copy of Florio's Montaigne at the British Museum, and joins in a publisher's supper fit for "a comical volume." Similar performances are staged on the Continent. Melville assists at "three comical comedies" in one evening in Paris, and, accompanied by Adler, goes to the "'Opera Comique' Boulevard des Italiens." He is entertained by "three vaudevilles" in Cologne and performs in "a few comical scenes" of his own with a landlady in Brussels. Back in London in mid-December, Melville is admitted to a pantomime rehearsal of *The Moon Queen and King Knight: or Harlequin Twilight,* and is introduced for the first time to the principal works of Sterne and De Quincey. He begins reading *Tristram Shandy,* that depiction of the mind's vagaries resulting in misunderstandings and confusions of speech, and, in a journey of one day, travels from cover to cover of the *Confessions of an English Opium-Eater,* a "most wondrous book."

Captain Fletcher, of the *Independence,* gives Melville yet another lesson in the relativity of perception when he asks his future passenger in London if he is a relative of Herman Melville. The fact that names sometimes coincide, thereby providing opportunity for misapprehension, stimulates the comic nerve in Melville, who the day before had gone to St. Thomas's Church to hear a sermon on charity by his "famous namesake (almost) 'The Reverend H Melvill.'" The famous author simply replies to the captain that yes, he is a relation of Herman Melville.[39] And, as though to prolong the joke for the entire voyage to Boston, Melville launches into a massive volume by Beaumont and the captain's namesake, Fletcher. He subsequently underscores in the tragicomedy *Philaster* lines reflecting the serious import of such merry playing: "The living . . . / . . . feed upon opinions, errours, dreams, / And make them truths" (3.1). Here is pictured the feast of life's confusion, the *comédie humaine* Melville has participated in as actor and spectator during his two-month stay away from home.

So located in a world of unreason, the truth-teller is fated to share in life's folly and error. It is a conundrum increasingly distressing to Melville. He writes to Evert Duyckinck from London on 14 December: "What a madness & anguish it is, that an author can never—under no conceivable circumstances—be at all frank with his readers.—Could I, for one, be frank with them—how would they cease their railing." The underlying cause of the anguish is suggested earlier in the letter: "I shall write such things as the Great Publisher of Mankind ordained ages before He published 'The World' . . ." (*ML* 1:347). The words make clear enough Melville's resolve to ignore the railing and incomprehension of his readers and to write those books he has been predestined to write. They also register his "passionate absolutism":[40] were he able to, he would speak the unequivocal verity which was directly apprehensible before the world's publication. In the face of that truth, all railing would cease. But the appetite for absolute knowledge cannot be satisfied, Melville must acknowledge, since God, by the very act of uttering truth indirectly, as in a book, had made frankness impossible. The human author is limited to seeking truth in mere reflections and to ciphering his discoveries by reflections of reflections. If some readers rail at the obliquity of his books, Melville rails at the obliquity of God's. Unlike those readers, though, he knows such railing to be futile. The fact is undeniable: the world has been published. It is for each reader, then, to divine for himself the truth of that publication. And since God's text signifies by indirection only, the insight its interpretation yields is inevitably uncertain and ambiguous. Not long after the arrival of the *Independence* at Boston in January 1850, Melville begins work on his sixth book, about a private and futile quest after the absolute as seen through the eyes of one man. *Moby-Dick,* an "endless sermon"[41] on the optics of relativity, takes for its ruling text a verse from the Holy Book: "For now we see through a glass darkly; but then face to face: now I know in part; but then shall I know even as also I am known" (1 Cor. 13:12).

Moby-Dick (1851) is at once a burlesque and an exegesis of the Pauline text in which Melville reads "the doubts of Montaigne" (*Mardi* 2:54).[42] "Here ye strike but splintered hearts together—there, ye shall strike unsplinterable glasses!"—so the sub-sub-librarian's scornful yet sympathetic commentator, in a company with "full eyes and empty glasses," proposes a toast to launch a bookish enterprise not to be taken "for veritable gospel cetology" (xii). Joining in the spirit of that toast, Ishmael's narrative tells of "glasses" specially designed to cheat drinkers (1:15) and recalls the confusion when a punch bowl is taken for a huge "finger-glass" (1:73). Outlandish punning of the kind establishes the iconoclasm of *Moby-Dick*, where St. Paul's glass is translated as a Narcissus mirror: if we see through a glass darkly, the book reflects, what we see there is our own face. Like a Narcissus mirror, this book growing out of the word *I*[43] images a pursuit after the "ungraspable phantom of life," which is the specter of the self (1:3–4). The roundabout chase of the self after the self, as the ancient myth cautions, is fraught with the danger of self-annihilation.

Like the Spanish doubloon nailed to the *Pequod*'s mainmast, the world is "a magician's glass" in which each man sees but himself, speculates Ishmael. Ahab, Starbuck, Flask, and others "read" the doubloon's "signs," and each interprets them differently, in accordance with his own lights and beliefs (2:190–91). The sun is "the only true lamp," insists the narrator—"all others but liars" (2:181). Of itself, the sun tells no lies. But, as refracted in men's eyes, the light it sends works to deceive: light is "the mystical cosmetic" (1:244). As Ishmael regrets with the Dutch metaphysical poet Jacob Revius,[44] "we are too much like oysters observing the sun through the water" (1:45). Readers of all signs, in books, whales, men, and nature, are victimized by the parallax and relativity of their private optic. Nor is the narrator himself exempt from error. Often self-deceived in his perceptions and inferences, Ishmael is caught up in "curious and contradictory speculations" (1:226). When in "The Affidavit" (chap. 45), for example, he swears that his "book" is "verity," he can produce but his own eyewitness testimony for a proof: "I say I, myself, have known" (1:254). *Testis unus, testis nullus.* A few pages later, he also confesses that "all sailors of all sorts are more or less capricious and unreliable" (1:266). Nor are the books he cites any more reliable, it would seem. His "best authorities" on cetology and other subjects are said either to confess their ignorance or to contradict each other (1:164, 263; 2:103).[45] In the world as a magician's glass each man reads his own nescience.

Each man reads but himself in the doubloon's mirror because the face itself of truth is absent there. What the Spanish coin says to its reader is what the "mirror" of the whale tells (2:2): "Thou shalt see my back parts, my tail, he seems to say, but my face shall not be seen" (2:123). The conceit speaks volumes. And when the leviathan's face does come into view, Ishmael pictures it as "a lipless, unfeatured blank" (2:352), "a dumb blankness full of meaning" (1:243). That dumbness is as undecipherable as the mystic writing seen through the "isinglass substance" covering the whale (2:31–32). It is a mystery perplexing to Ishmael and galling to his captain. "If the gods think to speak outright to man," Ahab protests, "they will honourably speak outright; not shake their heads and give an old wives' darkling hint" (2:341). Father Mapple is of another mind. The pilot-prophet clearly means no irony when, after spinning a yarn about Jonah based on "the opinion of learned men," he professes as his vocation, "To preach the Truth to the face of Falsehood": his task is "to sound . . . unwelcome truths" (1:51, 58). Had the preacher imitated the captain of his invention, however—the master of Jonah's vessel "rings every coin to find a counterfeit," as Father Mapple imagines (1:53)—he might have sounded another unwelcome Melvillean truth and seen the paradox in his role as "speaker of true things" (1:58): the face of Falsehood is all the Truth that man can read in the published books of this world.[46] Father Mapple seems to have taken at face value Montaigne's tongue-in-cheek description of imaginative preachers in "Des boyteux": "Quiconque croit quelque chose, estime que c'est ouvrage de charité de la persuader à un autre; et pour ce faire, ne craint poinct d'adjouster de son invention" (3.11.239).

In the absence of truth itself, man is left "to serpentine and spiralise" (2:171). "Stick to the boat" and "Leap from the boat" are aphorisms to illustrate such wisdom as is available to man, of the kind the fighting Quaker Bildad finds obscurely spelled in his Bible (2:168). "So man's insanity is heaven's sense," according to Ishmael's wry formulation (2:170). It is like the sense of the "awful Chaldee" inscribed on the sperm whale's brow, its "plaited . . . riddles" a "circle . . . impossible to square" (2:83–84). No reader or sage can escape "the whirl of woe" (1:54). "All men live enveloped in whale lines" (1:357), "plaited serpents" (2:29), "complicated coils" of rope (1:355) that cut like a "two-edged sword" (2:4). "The truest of all books is Solomon's, and Ecclesiastes is the fine hammered steel of woe. 'All is vanity.' ALL," reckons Melville's narrator, who, with Solomon, judges wisdom folly (2:181). The sage, like the narcissist, travels a circular course in his quest after truth. "We are turned round and round in this world" (2:330)—all suffer the fate of wounded sharks bending round, eating their own entrails, consuming and voiding themselves at once (2:26). Their self-annihilation imitates the self-cancellation of contradictory meanings pictured in both the mute blankness of the White Whale and the foolish wisdom of its students.[47]

The death of Ahab, then, is a grim mercy, putting an end to his whirl of woe. A promethean narcissist at war with himself—"a furious trope" has him turning a cannon on himself (1:231)—that "anaconda of an old man" (1:221) driven to revenge the wound that has left him unwhole is conclusively silenced by a coil of whale line about the neck. And the annihilation is not Ahab's alone. An appalling vortex finally pulls his ship and crew down to "hell" (2:367). Only Ishmael survives, an "orphan," in the last word of *Moby-Dick*. It is not that the solitary "I" who is the storyteller drifts in "an unFathered cosmos."[48] It is just that he has never seen his Father. Nor has he been able to find Him in the mirror of his Father's book or his own. What Ishmael has read there is himself; his Father absent, he has authored himself. As Melville asks in his own voice, "Why, ever since Adam, who has got to the meaning of this great allegory—the world?" (*ML* 1:435).

"Mad," "vague," and "indistinct" are qualifiers repeated in the minatory criticism which immediately greeted *Moby-Dick* (*ML* 1:437, 444–45, 446). More recent criticism has valued the epic differently, but with a faith implicitly as certain. "The book, like the coin, has remained finally inviolable," ends the foreword to *"Moby-Dick" as Doubloon: Essays and Extracts (1851–1970)*, as though to toast or revel in the radical instability of the text as revealed in the various and conflicting readings of Melville's book.[49] To do so, however, is to find more virtue and comfort than did Melville in the truth of narcissism mirrored in his work. After all, the voyage does end with the death of a ship, her captain, and all her crew save one. And even more appalling than such a conclusion is the torment of perpetual circumnavigation. With the end of each voyage survived another begins: "Such is the endlessness, yea, the intolerableness of all earthly effort," bewails Ishmael (1:73). His author had voiced a similar lament after finishing *Mardi* in 1849. While Melville senses with the near-completion of *Moby-Dick* that the unfolding within himself will soon reach the "inmost leaf" and that "shortly the flower must fall to the mould," as he confides to Hawthorne early in the summer of 1851, he again resolves to continue his dizzying chase after whole truth (*ML* 1:413). A month or so after the November publication of *Moby-Dick* in New York, Melville sets off on a voyage beginning where Ishmael's narration ends.

In less than six months, Melville completes *Pierre, or the Ambiguities* (1852), which represents the pursuit of truth as the search for a father's identity. His father dead many years, Pierre Glendinning has but portraits and hearsay by which to know him. The consuming need to see the reality behind these draws the youth into a world where right and wrong, fidelity and deceit, love and hate wear the same face. Neither the portraits of his father nor the words of the books Pierre desperately struggles to decode offer clear answers to his questions. "Qui ne coignoit pas Socrates, voyant son pourtraict, ne peut dire qu'il luy ressemble," as Montaigne writes, anticipating Pierre's perplexity (2.12.265). And when he attempts to unravel mystery by authoring a book of his own—he must "know what *is*" (90), "must see it face to face" (56)—Melville's quester, to his anguish, discovers that truth eludes "all verbal renderings" (155). What truth Pierre comes to see is but a "dark revealment" in his own "glass" (484), which revelation is further obscured by translation into the metaphors which are an author's words. The paradoxical conjunction of lying and truth-telling whirls Pierre round and round as in a "Maelstrom" (254). Only suicide brings his vertigo to an end.

"Blind moles" acting upon hints "eternally incapable of being cleared" (246, 275) is Melville's figure for humanity in *Pierre*. The knowledge necessary for a morally unambiguous life cannot be clearly apprehended because it comes to man by "dark similitude," "analogies . . . bitter to the thinker's belly" (57). Moral precepts are far from clear for another reason as well: "all the great books" which men consult for direction are "but mirrors, distortedly reflecting to us our own things" (395–96). Reflections of the contradictions in their readers, these books baffle in return. "The most immemorially admitted maxims of men . . . slide and fluctuate, and finally become wholly inverted," muses Pierre (231). His "exceedingly gentlemanly" father, for example, had taken it for a maxim that "all gentlemanhood was vain" (24, 6).[50] In this regard, man reflects the image of his Creator. "The lion and the lamb" embrace in the "glorious gospel" preached by a painting of that docile warrior, Pierre's grandfather. The old man, like his son, is pronounced a "fit image of his God" (39–40), for He, too, preaches by self-contradiction. The Holy Book, its code of revenge married to its code of love, calls on men to imitate both the serpent and the dove (143, 288–90). The thinkers of "all ages of the world," as Melville imagines, "pass as in a manacled procession" before such paradox (156). They are bound to circle in the darkness of unreason and folly.

If the paradox of truth as written impels the skeptical sage along a circle, however, that logic also compellingly argues for his silence, according to *Pierre*. Though "Solomon the Wise" did speak, what he spoke was, in a logical sense, nothing. "Eternally immovable" as it perfectly balances folly and wisdom, ignorance and enlightenment, Ecclesiastes is a massive blank stone, an "imaged muteness of the unfeatured heavens" (188–89, 153). "Hamletism" or "Memnon, Montaignised and modernised" (191) is the philosophy of unknowing Pierre reads in that musical stone, the doubter's permanent stillness at the balancing point of contradictory propositions. Poised between opposites, the sage is "dumb" by virtue of their mutual cancellation

(382). As the Book of Solomon asserts, "Silence is the only Voice of our God" (284). Since they are impossible to reconcile with each other, so Pierre infers, the contradictory teachings of the Bible are mute: their mystic speech, like music's, is inarticulate. All positive utterance of truth must consequently deceive. "This swindler's, this coiner's book," he reproaches his creation, thereby ironically confirming a publisher's opinion that the work is a "cheat" (498–99). "Be naught concealed in this book of sacred truth" (151), Melville writes, interrupting Pierre's narration, sardonically to remind the reader that sacred truth is ever a secret beyond the power of reason to understand and of words to say.

If Melville, like his protagonist, has cause to quarrel with God, he also has reason to quarrel with himself, for he also has published. Nor does the fact of self-conflict elude the author of *Pierre*. As though in mocking imitation of the shaped verses of such believers in the Logos or the Word as Porphyry and Herbert, Melville articulates his book of wisdom in twenty-six parts, to preach that man's alphabet can teach no certain truth and that the truly wise man, like the silent God he seeks or creates, is finally mute, a musical stone. The alphabet of *Pierre* fittingly ends with a play on words juggling with an act of self-annihilation. At the protagonist's beckoning, the two women he loves join him in suicide—a case of killing two birds with one stone, it is said (504). So a grotesque bilingual pun marks the conclusion of a youth's quest for truth and ends the joke of a book bent on silencing itself.

There is no record that Melville ever read the review of *Pierre* in *Godey's Lady's Book*. It was one of the few not to damn the novel outright as the ravings of a madman, more incomprehensible even than *Mardi* or *Moby-Dick*. But if he did, it must surely have brought a tortured smile to his lips. Supposing that the book has been offered in fun, as a burlesque of musical metaphysical speculation, the reviewer responds in a parody of its style: "in the insignificant significancies of that deftly-dealing and wonderfully-serpentining melodiousness, we have found an infinite, unbounded, inexpressible mysteriousness of nothingness" (*ML* 1:462). The jest nicely mimics the overwrought prose of a work that for more than five hundred pages insists on the impotence of language. In Melville's own words, from an 1854 story of another ineffectual invention, the theme and expression of *Pierre* are "inextricably interweaved together in one gigantic coil . . . like a huge nest of anacondas and adders."[51] Such tortuous elaboration suggests that Melville is played out in another sense as well: he had published five books in four years, including *Moby-Dick*. It will be almost two years after the completion of *Pierre* before Melville will publish another book-length fiction to challenge his uncomprehending readers and their faith.

Israel Potter (1855), Melville's eighth book, is a tale to teach the difference between faithful and unfaithful reading. The lesson begins with the dedication, "To His Highness The Bunker Hill Monument," where Melville's account of the author as interpreter sets a puzzle for readers who see merit only in fidelity to genuine fact. Appealing to the prejudice his reviewers had so often shown, Melville facetiously claims that his book preserves, "as in a reprint, Israel Potter's autobiographical story" (v). The story he refers to is the *Life and Remarkable Adventures of Israel R. Potter* (1824), a copy of which he had purchased in 1849. A moment's reflection, though, as Melville insinuates, will reveal the absurdity of such a claim, for no reading or writing can truly reproduce a book. To exact fidelity of the kind that requires an author to duplicate another's text is effectively to enjoin him to do nothing. Melville goes on to refine the irony. It is likely, he suggests, that even Israel R. Potter's words were not written by himself, "but taken down from his lips by another." Even that autobiography was but an interpretation, a "blurred record" of a life the authentic reality of which was literally "out of print" (v). Unfaithful though it is in the sense that it is not an exact duplicate, *Israel Potter* can accordingly claim a "general fidelity to the main drift of the original" (vi). It is true to the fact that the *Life and Remarkable Adventures of Israel R. Potter* is itself only a dark revelation by similitude, an imprecise translation of an autobiographer's genuine self. Melville therefore reckons that his work faithfully follows the chief injunction of "the Great Biographer," that man be faithful to "his Highness'" text. The "gloom" in the "closing chapters" of his own book, he forewarns, will be true to the main drift of that publication (vi). Like the gray Bunker Hill Monument and the balancing musical stone authored by Solomon the Wise in *Pierre*, the "tombstone" (vi) of *Israel Potter* will inscribe life's book as vanity and darkness.

"Be ye . . . wise as serpents, and harmless as doves" is Christ's command to His disciples as He sends them out to preach the gospel to the peoples of the world (Matt. 10:16). Melville's interpretation of the precept in *Israel Potter* argues that America has proved a zealous convert. Like the America he represents, the character Israel has "much of the gentleness of the dove" even as he is "not wholly without the wisdom of the serpent" (19). But unlike self-confident America and the comfortable Parson Falsgrave—in *Pierre* he dines wearing a brooch "representing the allegorical union of the serpent and dove" (143)—the Bunker Hill hero does not long remain unreflective before that paradox. When, in the role of a secret agent, he meets Benjamin Franklin in Paris, for example, Israel is mystified by the conjunction of "the apostolic serpent and dove" in the person, actions, and words of the sage (50–59). By contrast, the learned man of many parts knows no such perplexity. "God helps them that help themselves," Israel reads from *Poor Richard's Almanack* (69–70) and knows not exactly what to make of the inscrutable wisdom. He can no more understand Franklin's maxim than he can understand himself. Standing before a mirror reflecting the reversed letters of a foreign language, Israel puzzles over their meaning: "I wonder if I am right in my understanding of this alphabet?" (65). Shortly thereafter, he again finds himself facing that mirror, this time trying to unravel the "intertwisted ciphers" reflected from the tattoo on the inside of John Paul Jones's arm (81). That hieroglyphic, like the unthinking captain of the *Bon Homme Richard* who bears it, figures a mystifying union of refinement and savagery, simplicity and cunning. Israel cannot translate Jones any more clearly than he can read the self-image which the mirror returns.

The interchanging guises of ally and enemy that subsequently pass before Israel's eyes draw him deeper into reflection. His turbulent adventures at sea, where ships fly colors to deceive and where foe fires on foe and friend on friend, snare him in a circle—a "blank horizon, like a rope, coiled round the whole," as he becomes aware (206). One moment he is taken for a Yankee sailor, the next for a British tar. The reality ashore is no different. Like his fellow sufferers in "the City of Dis," the Yankee raising a family in a monarch's capital plods a "coiled thoroughfare," a prisoner of endless ambiguity: "all faces" in London are "more or less snowed or spotted with soot" (212). "What signifies who we be?" he comes to ask himself before "the contradictions of human life" (206, 216). The answer, Israel concludes, is that he, like every other man, is "nobody" (209), a nullity of multiple and contradictory identities and opposite valences. "All is vanity" (206, 209). And what the eponymous patriot's story writes in small, America, a nation of contradictions gathering in itself all the peoples of the world, ciphers in large. An analogue of the book of America and the sacred text translated there as a union of serpent and dove, the Old Testament and the New, the book of Israel Potter's life takes its author and reader full circle. Returning to his place of origin after a half-century exile, the pilgrim meditates on the round of his life—"the ends meet" (225)—and judges it an empty, incomprehensible dream, a vanity. The cycle of paradox, once closed, traces nothing. So ends the journey of this reader of enigmatic texts.

As Melville had cause to anticipate, the somber allegory of *Israel*

Potter fell largely on deaf ears. Reviews like the one in *Putnam's Monthly Magazine* (May 1855) sustained Melville's conviction that readers had not learned much from him in the years since *Typee* and *Omoo*. "It has sometimes been inquired," observes the critic, "whether . . . *Israel Potter* is a romance or an authentic narrative." A comparison of the book with its original conclusively demonstrates that it is a romance (*ML* 1:501). But the review misses the point of the book, that all narrative is translation and that no translation can be completely true to its original. The commentator seems not to have read the bottom line of Melville's thesis: that the application of such a critical method to the Holy Book must show that it, too, is a romance. If readers have not learned from Melville's skepticism, he has learned much from theirs. The fact that such impercipience appeared on the pages of the very magazine that had initially set *Israel Potter* before the public (July 1854–March 1855) further serves to measure the distance between Melville and the reader of his day. Even his publisher had not faithfully read the author he had put in print. In the fall of 1855, Melville begins what will prove to be his last serious effort to make himself understood. The Bible will not serve as analogue or subtext in *The Confidence-Man*. It will be re-created as a character speaking with the voice of Melville, to teach what constitutes for him a faithful reading of God's publications and his own books. No double standard for the author of *Israel Potter:* his words and the Bible's have equal authority.

The Confidence-Man sets out by introducing two characters, the Bible and America. First to appear is a lamblike deaf-mute who traces on a slate words from 1 Corinthians (13:4–8) calling for faith and charity. The words provoke indignation and derision among the passengers of the *Fidèle,* a steamer departing St. Louis for New Orleans on April Fools' Day. They sense a kind of "lunacy" in the "singularity" of the "singularly innocent" writer—the man is evidently a "simpleton" (2–3). What the passengers fail to see is that the mute's words are an imposture, confidently presenting as literally simple the truth of a book that is set before the reader of *The Confidence-Man* as a multiplying and ambiguous mirror. Had the mute continued to copy St. Paul's epistle, his readers would have heard that truth cannot be seen with clarity and certainty in this world: we see *per speculum in aenigmate*. The diagraming of paradox by the juxtaposition of opposite propositions—"Charity believeth all things" next to the sign hanging over a barber-shop door, "NO TRUST"—perplexes the passengers of the *Fidèle*.[52] The faithful reader of the Bible, so the first chapter of *The Confidence-Man* insinuates, should be similarly perplexed. Is not the Holy Book counseling both "charity and prudence" (38) itself a double-talking confidence man, the work of an artist?

The America Melville sets afloat in the second chapter, "Showing that Many Men have Many Minds," is similarly paradoxical. Gathered from all the kinds of "that multiform pilgrim species, man," the passengers of the *Fidèle* constitute a congress of opposites. "Fine ladies in slippers and moccasined squaws . . . Quakers in full drab, and United States soldiers in full regimentals . . . Mormons and Papists . . . jesters and mourners . . . grinning negroes, and Sioux chiefs as solemn as high priests"—these are but a few of the characters in this parliament of God's plenty (6), "the home of man," in the words of Emerson's "The Young American."[53] Uniting "the most distant and opposite zones," the cool North and the warm South, they sweep along, like the Mississippi, "in one cosmopolitan and confident tide" (6). *Mardi* had imagined a similar reconciliation of opposites, but only as a divine comedy: "grim Dante" and "fat Rabelais" laughing together, "monk Luther" and "Pope Leo" embracing, and the differences between "the Stagirite and Kant . . . forgotten" (1:14). Only in heaven are enigma and absurdity dispelled by the effulgence of whole truth. And America is not heaven yet, as the harlequin playing of *The Confidence-Man* suggests, locating America as it does in a secular All Fools' Day distantly removed from the Feast of All Saints. Confusions multiply aboard the *Fidèle* as she steams between "vine-tangled" banks and her passengers offer conflicting interpretations of the mute's meaning (5). America's sweeping self-assurance, then, is chimerical: her confidence is the effect of blindness to the irreconcilable contradictions within herself and in the Holy Book of which she acts as a type. Both are earthly publications and consequently enigmatic texts more encouraging of darkness and doubt than certainty and light. America, like the Melvillean version of the Bible, is paradox and a deception in *The Confidence-Man*, pressing on the world her claim to heavenly enlightenment even as she is filled with contradiction and obscurity.

In chapter 14, "Worth the Consideration of Those to Whom It May Prove Worth Considering," Melville explains his own participation in folly and enigma as a reader and writer of these two characters. Since *Mardi*, he had attempted to convey to readers his sense of the obscurity at the heart of existence. Since *Mardi*, they had taxed him with obscurity. Now, in his own voice, he states plainly what he had so often hinted at before. Even "the acutest sage," Melville writes, is "often at his wits' ends to understand living character" (58). What is said of "the divine nature" applies to the "human": "in view of its contrasts," he proposes, its truth is "past finding out" (59). It follows that the lineaments of those natures are painted with the least avoidable injustice by an author who does not represent them "in a clear light" (59). The bafflingly variegated guises of a character, like those of the novel's devilish confidence man, should make him seem all the more convincing and genuine. Only slightly less overt is Melville's rider that the very act of literary (re)creation is true to life. Since a "living character" is not the being in itself but the being as read by others, the representation of "mere phantoms which flit along a page, like shadows along a wall" (58), conforms to what is already a fact of quotidian life. And, extending this line of argument, Melville goes on to raise the objection that the youth who reads novels for wisdom reads false maps. Certainly, the young man would not aimlessly wander in untruth were he "furnished with a true delineation" (60). But an accurate map of the heart of man is no more available to readers than is a true delineation of the divine living character. This being so, Melville argues, the deceiving cartography of *The Confidence-Man* is conformal with the reality of man's nescience and folly. The justification of his own work rests, at bottom, on the analogy he draws between the Holy Book and his own. Both are enigmatic, both fabulous in his eyes. The final inference Melville leaves to his lector: to criticize obscurity in his book is ultimately to fault the darkness of his Maker's.

There is much that is old in Melville's line of reasoning here. John Bunyan, for example, had similarly argued in defense of *The Pilgrim's Progress,* a major source for *The Confidence-Man.* In "The Author's Apology for His Book," Bunyan admits that "metaphors make us blind" and that books speak in "feigning words." His initial conclusion: rather publish not at all than publish lies. But the author immediately sets his logic to naught: God himself has authorized publication. The "dark and cloudy" words of Bunyan's book but follow the example of Holy Writ, "everywhere . . . full of all these things, / Dark Figures, allegories."[54] The analogy between the two scriptures finally collapses into a virtual identity when *The Pilgrim's Progress* takes for its epigraph a verse from Hosea, "I have used similitudes" (12:10), words voiced by "The Lord God." So far, Melville agrees.

But the author of *The Confidence-Man* pursues the argument further. When Bunyan professes that from the dark figures of the Bible come "rays / Of light that turns our darkest night into days,"[55] Melville dissents. From darkness comes darkness, which thesis an ironic reading of *The Pilgrim's Progress* itself might sustain. When its author pictures Christian in Vanity Fair, for example, listening to gossip about citizens of the Town of Fair-Speech—Mr. Smooth-Man,

Mr. Facing-both-ways, Mr. Two-tongues, and Lady Feigning—[56] it is as though Bunyan the Christian were listening to stories about Bunyan the author of feigning words. Two-tongued himself, he is snared in the contradiction of telling truth by telling lies. Seen from a Melvillean point of vantage, Bunyan is a bona fide citizen of Vanity Fair and an obedient servant to its chief lord Beelzebub, the master of all equivocators and confidence men. "I have formerly lived by hearsay and faith, but now I go where I shall live by sight," Bunyan ends "The Conclusion" as he senses death's approach. By his own admission, so *The Confidence-Man* as impious gloss may be read to argue, the author of *The Pilgrim's Progress* has been a blind man leading the blind. Frank Goodman, the demonic Cosmopolitan and confidence man, will similarly translate the Pauline text by blowing out the light of Holy Writ and leading a student of the Bible into total darkness.

The Confidence-Man, like *Moby-Dick*, burlesques the scripture concluding *The Pilgrim's Progress*. This time, though, the playing has as its object the unmasking of hypocrisy. When Frank Goodman asks the barber Cream whether he would trust a man he had seen only from behind, for example, the answer is yes; but when asked whether he would trust that same man in darkness, "where his face would remain unseen," Cream answers no (195). The barber, however, seems to have confidence in the Bible. That inconsequence and the double standard it practices had earlier been set before the reader by Mr. Truman, satanic agent for the Black Rapids Coal Company, when he damns the bears of the stock market as "hypocrites in the simulation of things dark instead of bright" (41). His ambiguous syntax imputes hypocrisy to those who look into the dark mirror of the Holy Book and see in that simulacrum of truth nothing but light. The Bible, according to Melville's iconoclastic rendition, is not less enigmatic than *The Confidence-Man*. Both are made to baffle more than enlighten.[57] It follows that those who trust in Holy Writ as a builder of confidence but withhold their confidence from words fashioned in that book's image are hypocrites. The reader faithful to the design of *The Confidence-Man*, on the other hand, will divine that St. Paul, like his imitator Melville, is numbered there among "the destroyers of confidence" (41).

If anything is clear from *The Confidence-Man* it is that similitudes read in a dark mirror enlighten not at all. For Melville, analogy is the "dubious medium" of the "equivocator" (112–13). The parable of China Aster, a candle-maker who finishes his days in gloom, serves as illustration: two characters interpret the story, and each draws from it a lesson opposite to the other's (189–91). An "analogy" is a "pun with ideas" (107), a prank to send the thinking man into a spin. Additionally, in accordance with Bunyan's formulation, analogy is a form of hearsay, which notion impels much of the dark hilarity of *The Confidence-Man*, as in this vertiginous sequence of translations: Mr. Ringman tells the story of the "enigma" Goneril to a merchant; the story is then elaborated and substantiated by a man in gray (Ringman in disguise) as it is transmitted to Mr. Roberts; and it is subsequently reworded by the author for the benefit of his readers while Mr. Roberts tells the story to Mr. Truman, who is Mr. Ringman, the confidence man in yet another of his guises. This last listener doubts the veracity of Mr. Roberts's retelling (51–54). Like the parable of China Aster, the story of Goneril invites contradictory readings. Again, similar doubts are raised by the chronicle of Colonel Moredock (chaps. 26–28). The account of the loving and vengeful Indian-hater shows the amplification of distortion attendant on history's transmission through generations.[58] Frank Goodman suggests that the story is dubious for another reason as well: "some parts don't hang together." Surely, he objects, a history uniting the "man of hate" and the "man of love" is of uncertain credit (136). Melville's hint is not so very hidden: the Bible should likewise inspire incredulity in the heedful reader. Readers, beware of similitudes and unreason wherever they are found.

How far Melville finally pressed the analogy he saw between his own enigmatic scripture and the Holy Guide-Book is shown in the conclusion of *The Confidence-Man*. In chapter 8, he had introduced a widow holding a small gilt Testament, her fingers inserted at 1 Corinthians 13. The "sacred page no longer meets her eye" as she looks to the western hills, to that fading light that lingers "though the sun be set" (37–38). There is no clear light for her in St. Paul, who counsels both "charity and prudence" (38). Nor is there illumination in 1 Corinthians 13 for the author of *The Confidence-Man*. In the end, Melville is faithful to the darkness and contradiction he reads everywhere in the Bible. When Frank Goodman, a reader of "Hume on suicide" (117), blows out the solar lamp ringed with two alternating figures representing the Old Testament and the New, he merely confirms what, for Melville, is Holy Writ's and Wisdom's self-extinction. The contrary valences of lamb and lion, dove and serpent, articles of war and articles of love—these finally annihilate each other in his eyes. What remains is an obscurity akin to Hell's, a world "mute of all light," as Dr. John Carlyle translates from Dante's *Inferno*.[59]

As Melville will write in "The Conflict of Convictions," composed near the beginning of the internecine war between North and South, "WISDOM IS VAIN, AND PROPHESY." Wisdom is vain because God, like the balancing skeptic and the infernal confidence man, speaks in a diabolic tongue, by paradox. He neither simply affirms nor denies:

> YEA AND NAY—
> EACH HATH HIS SAY:
> BUT GOD HE KEEPS THE MIDDLE WAY.

And prophecy is vain because the face of God is nowhere to be seen, veiled as it is by the hearsay or similitude which is his published creation:

> NONE WAS BY
> WHEN HE SPREAD THE SKY
>
> (*Poems*, 10)

"Was Man . . . present at the Creation . . . to see how it all went on? Have any deepest scientific individuals yet dived-down to the foundations of the Universe, and gauged everything there?" Carlyle, echoing the voice of God (Job 38), had asked in *Sartor Resartus*, to the humbling of human reason.[60] But if science has not brought to light the "groundplan of the incomprehensible All,"[61] neither has the seer or poetic sage, is Melville's response. Standing before the mirror of God's works, the Bible, the World, and Man, the Melvillean seeker after wisdom reads nothing but silence and absence. That is what the divine scriptures have to teach him in the end. And so concludes the scripture of *The Confidence-Man*: "Something further may follow of this Masquerade." What follows is nothing, or "la franchise du silence" such as Montaigne had recommended to would-be seers lost in ignorance (3.5.63). Not for Melville the inconsequence of the Sage of Concord. The man who speaks "as books enable . . . babbles. Let him hush," Emerson had taught in the Harvard Divinity School Address of July 1838, and had continued to lecture and write books for the public good.[62] Melville agrees and hushes. That silence was all the truth that remained for the blind pilot-prophet to teach. Melville's circling paradoxical art had consumed itself, finally.

Epilogue

Melville did publish after *The Confidence-Man*—but in verse only, and more for private than for public circulation. His volume of poems on the Civil War appeared in 1866, repeating the conclusion he had reached a decade before. "The turmoil and final nothingness of the understanding," words he underscores in a copy of Hazlitt's *The*

Round Table (*ML* 2:711), summarize his theme.[63] A decade later, G. P. Putnam's & Sons published *Clarel,* anonymously and at Melville's own expense. The spiritual autobiography in some 18,000 lines of iambic tetrameter took its inspiration from his visit to Europe and the Levant shortly after the completion of *The Confidence-Man.* As *Clarel* tortuously explained, the pilgrimage had not led to a new faith: "dumb argument / Expressive more than words" (2:283), articulates what wisdom Melville gleaned from the sun-drenched Holy Land. The poem is an "enigma" with "no logical course or . . . any distinct conclusions" (*ML* 2:750)—so a reviewer dismissed *Clarel* in June 1876, in much the same manner in which America had dismissed *The Confidence-Man* some twenty years before.[64] For Melville, nothing much has changed: there is nothing new under the sun.[65] But he seems no longer much concerned whether anyone is listening or not. "I here dismiss the book—content beforehand with whatever future awaits it," ends the author's note to *Clarel.* His next work, *John Marr,* was privately printed in September 1888, in twenty-five copies. In November of that year, Melville began the prose *Billy Budd,* which, in its apparently unfinished form three years later, would wait more than thirty years for publication. This ambiguous tale of the Articles of War and the Sermon on the Mount was to invite such contradictory interpretations as to corroborate Melville's final testament of silence.[66] *Billy Budd* appropriately ends with the words of a dead sailor forever encoiled: "I am sleepy and the oozy weeds about me twist." In February 1891, Melville began reading Schopenhauer's *Counsels and Maxims,* and purchased two additional volumes by that author, *The World as Will and Idea* and *The Wisdom of Life.* The philosopher's dreamy Eastern wisdom found a congenial reader. *Timoleon,* privately printed in April of that year, includes the poem "Buddha," with its epigraph in the spirit of Ecclesiastes. "Nirvana! absorb us in your skies, / Annul us into thee," ends Melville's prayer. What he fervently looked forward to in life he had already achieved in fiction. "A flame to melt—a wind to freeze," "love and hate"—these opposites "meet and mate" in his art, as he reflects in the poem immediately preceding "Buddha."[67] There is, then, a kind of poetic justice in the last sentence of the notice that appeared in *The Press* (New York) on 29 September 1891, the day after Melville's death: "Probably, if the truth were known, even his own generation has long thought him dead, so quiet have been the later years of his life" (*ML* 2:836). The blind sage and artist had come to a "nirvana," literally a blowing out or an extinction of light, some thirty years before, with the conclusion of *The Confidence-Man: His Masquerade.*

4
Of Blindness in Conrad's Spectacular Universe

> Les cartes sont si meslées . . . qu'il est malaisé d'y eviter confusion et desordre.
> —Montaigne, "De la conscience"

> Our eyes were of no more use to us than if we had been buried miles deep in a heap of cotton-wool.
> —Conrad, *Heart of Darkness*

IN April 1891, some four months after Captain Józef Konrad Korzeniowski's return to Europe from the Congo with the still unfinished manuscript of his first novel, *Almayer's Folly* (pub. 1895), Herman Melville received the privately printed twenty-five copies of his last completed work, *Timoleon*. Included in the slim volume is a reflection on the interior struggle which is the process of literary creation. Melville writes in "Art":

> In placid hours well pleased we dream
> Of many a brave unbodied scheme.
> But form to lend, pulsed life create,
> What unlike things must meet and mate:
> A flame to melt—a wind to freeze;
> Sad patience—joyous energies;
> Humility—yet pride and scorn;
> Instinct and study; love and hate;
> Audacity—reverence. These must mate
> And fuse with Jacob's mystic heart,
> To wrestle with the angel—Art.[1]

Though the hours of visionary dreaming preparatory to artistic creation will often prove to be far from pleasant or placid for Joseph

Conrad—"I am sunk in a vaguely uneasy dream of visions of innumerable tales that float in an atmosphere of voluptuously aching bones," as a letter of May 1905 pictures[2]—he, too, will describe the grammar ruling the human heart, the visible universe there contained, and the art of rendering justice to that universe as "the intimate alliance of contradictions."[3] And, like Melville, Conrad will conceive of the imagination's activity as a struggling with inscrutable powers, in the solitude of a great darkness.

"The strain of a creative effort," Conrad writes in Part 5 of *A Personal Record* (1912), is materially paralleled "in the *everlasting sombre stress* of the westward winter passage round Cape Horn. For that too is the wrestling of men with the might of their Creator, in a great isolation from the world" (98–99; emphasis added). Like the endless tension experienced by mariners toiling in the icy waters off Tierra del Fuego, the act of literary creation is inconclusive travail in a turbulent element rife with ambiguity and mystery. Conrad might have added yet another parallel, in the stress of the westward winter passage round the Cape of Good Hope as imagined in his first deep-sea fiction, *The Nigger of the "Narcissus."* In the dark and stormy solitude of a numbing sea, the blinded mariners of the *Narcissus* suffer a trial analogous to their author's: "In an unendurable and unending strain they worked like men driven by a merciless dream to toil in an atmosphere of ice or flame. They burnt and shivered in turns" (92–93).[4] The crew of the *Judea* similarly suffers in *Youth,* their "incessant" turning at the pumps in pitch darkness or clouds of sulphurous smoke, "a hell for sailors," serving not only as "a symbol of existence," but of art as well (4, 12). The artist's travail in a zone of ambiguity is unmistakably hellish, as the more obviously metafictive *Heart of Darkness* corroborates: "I sweated and shivered over that business . . . hot and cold all over," Marlow recalls his bedevilment as a "blindfolded" master navigating the serpentine Congo River, his sight obscured as much by bright mist as by darkness (94). What truth the tale of Marlow's vortical odyssey in "the gloomy circle of some Inferno" tells (66), Conrad's "The Ascending Effort" (1910) states as a matter of fact: "Life and the arts follow dark courses, and will not turn aside to the brilliant arc-lights of science" (*Notes on Life and Letters,* 74).

Because of the invincible obscurity of the underlying truth it strives to bring to light, so the 1897 Preface to *The Nigger of the "Narcissus"* establishes, art cannot help men fit themselves for "the hazardous enterprise of living." "The aim of creation cannot be ethical at all," Conrad goes on to propose in Part 5 of *A Personal Record*. Observation of the unreason ruling the visible universe in all its aspects—"this earth [is] the abode of conflicting opinions," a playhouse of absurdities and contradictions in which one foolish wisdom demolishes another—argues that the object of art is "purely spectacular," "to bear true testimony . . . to the supreme law and the abiding mystery of the sublime spectacle" (92). All creation testifies that "imagination . . . is the supreme master of art as of life," and that the enigmatic spectacle which the literary imagination attempts precisely to mirror is "a moral end in itself" (25, 93). The dreaming Schopenhauer and his long-sleeper Montaigne nod their agreement: the artist's "true, deep knowledge of the inner nature of the world . . . [is] an end in itself."[5] The artist makes no appeal to surface reason, "that part of our being which is . . . dependent on wisdom," as Conrad's preface of 1897 asserts. Rather, he follows the dark course of the imagination, and descends within himself, "into the abyss of infernal regions," that lonely place of "cold fire," in the words of *Victory* (219, 375). It is there, in the obscure life of the emotions and their roundabout logic, that he finds the terms of his appeal. "Extremes touch," *A Personal Record* renders the spectacular artist's creed (132).[6]

"To see! to see!—this is the craving . . . of blind humanity," by Conrad's reckoning in 1906, in *The Mirror of the Sea* (87). Nor is the artist's hunger for enlightenment less keen. His task is to see the truth of the universe of stress and strife that humanity creates and suffers, and, by the emotional power of the written word, to make others see that truth. But, like the "contradictory beams" of Pandora's torch in *La estatua de Prometeo*,[7] Calderón's figure for the imagination's power simulated in Kurtz's painting of a blindfolded woman carrying a torch in darkness (*Heart of Darkness*, 79), the artist's ambiguous illumination blurs rather than clarifies ethical distinctions, and so leaves humanity just as it finds it, groping in a moral obscurity. The underlying truth which art is empowered to convey is the reality of that blindness, that each individual is isolated as in a hellish dream. The artist, it follows, is one of us: his is "the subtle conviction of solidarity . . . in dreams," according to the credo prefacing Conrad's first tale of communal narcissism on the high seas. What, then, can one know or see in a universe impenetrable to reason? "*Chi lo sà?*" the author of *A Personal Record* answers before a Cimmerian spectacle such as had reduced Montaigne to infinite puzzlement and Melville to silence (93).

Conrad's art never aims at "moral justification or condemnation of conduct" (*The Arrow of Gold*, 4). He is not to be taken for "a sage," as he warns in "A Familiar Preface" to *A Personal Record*. It is not his business "to write in order to reprove mankind for what it is, or praise it for what it is not, or—generally—to teach it how to behave."

This artist, Conrad reminds his reader, writes only "about himself" and "the twilight of life" he sees mirrored in that private abyss, where "joy and sorrow . . . pass into each other, mingling their forms." Perhaps with Arnold's description of Emerson as a latter-day "Roman Emperor Marcus Aurelius" in mind,[8] he emphasizes that "the counsels of Marcus Aurelius are not for me. They are more fit for a moralist than for an artist" (xiii–xvi). Here as elsewhere, Conrad makes no secret of his scorn for gospel preachers of all kinds. As he remarks in "Autocracy and War" (1905), sages who peer into "a bottomless abyss" and find "ground" or "footing" there for doctrines of wisdom and salvation "present a sight of alarming comicality" (*Notes on Life and Letters*, 101, 108). More gently in the "Author's Note" to the volume that includes "Autocracy and War," he tweaks those readers who would look to his own work for some kind of practical and logically coherent doctrine: "There will be plenty of people sagacious enough to perceive the absence of all wisdom from these pages" (vii). "Facing imperturbably all the conflicting impulses of human nature," as Edward Garnett distinguishes Conrad from his English contemporaries, he holds neither openly nor secretly "an ethical belief."[9] He remains ever impartial before the comedy of the absurd that is life.

"Les autres [les moralistes] forment l'homme; je le recite et en represente un particulier bien mal formé," Montaigne opens "Du repentir" (3.2.20). Though never one to show himself in public *en pantoufles*, Conrad similarly distinguishes his private enterprise from the sage's; and, like the Renaissance master of ethical indifference, he locates life and art in a zone of "impalpable grayness," "a sickly atmosphere of tepid scepticism" (*Heart of Darkness*, 150–51), "[une] obscurité si espesse et inextricable, qu'on n'y peut rien choisir de son avis" (*Essais* 2.12.173). According to Edward E. Said's apt suggestion, "Truth for Conrad was . . . the negation of intellectual differentiation."[10] Everything, it is certain, comes to look pretty much the same with the approach of darkness. Convinced that "we live, as we dream—alone" (*Heart of Darkness*, 82) and that no man can see more clearly than his private light permits in that twilight existence, the Conradian artist tasked with making men see the truth of life can speak but obscurely and inconclusively, in a "diabolic tongue."[11] His language, like Kurtz's in *Heart of Darkness*, befuddles by its double-speaking, leaving the reader suspended in ambiguity, as between darkness and light: "the gift of expression . . . bewildering . . . illuminating, [is] the most exalted and the most contemptible, the pulsating stream of light, or the deceitful flow from the heart of an impenetrable darkness" (113–14). The gifted rhetorician may indeed provide "practical hints" on occasion, but only by a non sequitur compatible with the capricious and contradictory logic of his art. Kurtz's final written directive—"Exterminate all the brutes!"—is exemplary in this regard: it comes "like a flash of lightning in a serene sky" (118).

"The formulas of art," Conrad generalizes in *Notes on Life and Letters*, "are dependent on things variable, unstable, and untrustworthy" (5–6). Only a fool would take an unstable helmsman for a trustworthy guide, as Marlow ironically reflects in *Heart of Darkness*, itself "a story that strangely moves in two quite opposite directions":[12] "I take it, no fool ever made a bargain for his soul with the devil" (117). Kurtz's last disciple, the Russian Sailor said to be "full of mystery and wisdom," is just such a fool: "He looked like a harlequin" (122–23). Charmed as by a snake, the disciple in motley takes in his master's "splendid monologues . . . on love, justice, conduct of life—or what not" and believes in their wisdom, though he can make neither head nor tail of what they say (132). The sight of a student imbibing wisdom at the knees of Conrad's art of unknowing offers a spectacle of similar comicality.

Heart of Darkness, writes C. B. Cox, is "a great parable concerning, among other things, the role of the artist in modern times."[13] But if a parable, it is one of the modern kind. It is not a short, simple story, usually of an occurrence of a familiar kind, from which a moral lesson can be drawn. Understandably, Conrad's commentators are hard pressed to say what lesson(s) his double-speaking art teaches, other than that "the darkness will never reveal the ultimate source of its mystery."[14] As a recent study summarizes the joke of Conrad's spectacular parables of indifference, which offer no kernel of meaning, "nothing" is what "we are to comprehend more fully" from them in the end.[15] The Victorian sages Carlyle and Emerson, their minds, like Teufelsdröckh's, "drawn two ways at once" and their eyes divining "strong sunshine in weeping skies" (or, conversely, weeping skies in sunshine),[16] had made as much known.

For Conrad, the artist who would be sage represents a droll contradiction. The devilishly ambiguous Conradian rhetorician with a disciple in motley is an elusive purveyor of moonshine of the kind Nabokov will set playing in the tutorial dream of Professor Charles Kinbote, who names Gide "the Lucid" and whose own circular thinking, figured by the wheel of a car endlessly spinning in snow as it forms "a concave inferno of ice," shows him kin to that goliard.[17] Heir to the wise man Montaigne had observed authoring a foolish book (that is, himself), the harlequin artist in the guise of a sage is a fit subject for comic diversion: "l'artizan et sa besoigne se contrarient"

(*Essais* 3.2.21). Such a confounding of incompatible vocations, however, can have fatal results for those who take it seriously, as Conrad points out in the essay "Outside Literature" (1922). Contrary to "Notices to Mariners," that "most trusted kind of printed prose" because written in scrupulously precise "unliterary language" that speaks "simply" and does not "plumb the depths," imaginative literature is inherently fickle and perfidious: "An imaginatively written Notice to Mariners would be a deadly thing. I mean it literally. It would be sure to kill a number of people." Because of its radical instability and indeterminacy, the subjectivity of its vision and the duplicity of its language, "a dreadful doubt hangs over the whole achievement of literature." It is a prose, not of "Responsibility," but of "mystification" and "Speculation," inviting conflicting interpretations and deadly confusion (*Last Essays*, 39–43). R. B. Cunninghame Graham's reckoning in the 1925 preface to *Tales of Hearsay* implicitly confirms the artist's warning that his work is not to be trusted: Conrad locates himself and his reader in "a ship fogbound off a dangerous coast."[18] If so, best that the imaginative writer not lead at all and that his public not be led. Teufelsdröckh's advice, given in a moment of concern for practical matters and much at his own expense, is apposite: "When the blind lead the blind, both shall fall into the ditch; wherefore, in such circumstances, may it not sometimes be safer, if both leader and led simply—sit still?"[19] "*Memento mori*," the writer of Notices to Mariners is bidden never to forget (*Last Essays*, 41). It is otherwise with the artist, who appeals to what is capricious in man. Those who take him for a sage, then, do so foolishly and at their own peril. With a fool as a guide, they travel blind, in unending circles.

The qualities of the man fit to serve as a ship's master are cognate with the characteristics of the prose of responsibility and those which "fit us best for the hazardous enterprise of living." Conrad sets out these qualities in a letter of February 1891 to Marguerite Poradowska, shortly after his return to London from the Congo. He hopes to have the command of one of M. Pécher's steamers, and tells his aunt that there are no impediments to his being so entrusted. An English Master's Certificate testifies to his competence in the lore of the sea; and, as letters of reference from shipowners can attest, he is a sober, law-abiding individual, stable and not given to the caprices of passion. He can be trusted. But the rhetoric of the emotionally charged letter testifies that the author of the unfinished manuscript of *Almayer's Folly* has what it takes to become a writer of the imagination, of the untrustworthy prose of mystification and speculation. Perhaps half-expecting his hope of getting the command to come to nothing,

Conrad seems ironically to mock the very expectation to which his letter gives voice. And when he goes on to tell Marguerite Poradowska that he does suffer from certain physical ailments, but not of the kind to disqualify him from taking on the responsibility of a ship's master, Conrad expresses himself in a complex double allusion: "Il est vrai que je boîte, mais je suis en compagnie distinguée. Timoléon était boîteux et il y a même un diable qui l'est d'après ce que j'ai entendu dire."[20] Though the likely source of the second allusion, Alain-René Lesage's satirical novel *Le Diable boîteux (1707; The Devil upon Two Sticks)*, may come readily enough to mind, the sense of the mariner's association of himself with Lesage's devil is far from clear, since Timoleon was sound of limb.

A simple error dispels any mystery here for the editors of the collected letters: "Conrad confuses Timoleon, the Greek statesman, with Tamurlane, the lame conqueror."[21] If, however, Conrad writes what he means and means what he writes, that "Timoléon était boîteux," using the term as Montaigne does in "Des boyteux," to figure, in accordance with Plutarch's observation, humanity's growing infirmity in a universe darkening as it grows older (3.11.237), the mariner's comparison is grimly ironic. Timoleon, in fact, was "lame": according to Plutarch's life of the Greek statesman and commander of fleets and armies, his sight grew so weak with age that he finished his days blind.[22] As Conrad will write a decade later, in *The End of the Tether*, published together with *Heart of Darkness* and *Youth* in 1902, "A ship's unseaworthy when her captain can't see" (300). Nor is the devilishly playful ironist the man to be trusted with writing Notices to Mariners. Recollection of the fact that the Greeks of Sicily sought the blind Timoleon's direction in all difficult and important matters of state, and, always and unanimously, followed his unerring guidance, only serves further to bewilder the reader who takes Conrad's comparison of himself with Timoleon in 1891 as no slip of the pen.

Whether a simple mistake or a vaguely calculated manifold irony in the letter to Marguerite Poradowska *(chi lo sà?)*, the confounding of a man shaky on his legs with one who cannot see is no accident in Conrad's *The End of the Tether*. In this tale of a blind captain who postures as a sighted man, of a fool wearing "an air of profound wisdom" (290), Mr. Van Wyk, a would-be friend to the master of the *Sofala*, seduces the ship's first mate into acceding to what they both know is a lie, that Captain Whalley's legs are giving out. The lie figures the central duplicity about which the entire tale is spun: *The End of the Tether* turns on the deadly treachery of agents of ignorance who pose as qualified sages and luminaries. In Conrad's eyes, there can be no clear and discernible ethical purpose in the purely spectacular universe, since imagination, not reason, is the capricious master of both art and life; and inscrutable Chance, their ruling deity.

Plutarch's description of the agency of Chance in his *Life of Timoleon*, an exemplum of the man favored by hidden powers in all his enterprises, suggests how well fitted she is to personify the imagination's dark workings in the universe of Conrad's fiction: "The goddess Chance uses one event to give rise to another, brings together those farthest removed from each other, and intermingles those which seem most different and to have nothing in common, by so disposing them that the end of the one begins the other."[23] Time and again, Timoleon prevailed against all odds; and even his blindness, Plutarch confidently affirms, proved a blessing: "Chance did not play him a dirty trick."[24] Timoleon never pretended to understand the logic of her ways. He trusted to Chance, and, happily, she never played him false. In the *Life of Timoleon*, it is man and not the goddess who is blind, for her mysterious dispositions prove themselves wonderfully sagacious and constructive in their effects. As recounted by the first-century Greek moralist, Timoleon's life is a "mysterious arrangement of . . . logic," but not of the "merciless" kind working "for a futile purpose" (*Heart of Darkness*, 150). It is otherwise in the tale of Captain Whalley. As though ironically to complete a Plutarchian diptych, the life of Conrad's dim-eyed mariner bound for disaster returns an inverted image of Timoleon's. There is bad luck, too, and art empty of ethical purpose. Neither the unfortunate Whalley nor his author is able to see more clearly into the logic of existence than is permitted by the hidden unreason raveling "some endless and jocose dream" in *Heart of Darkness* (131). Like the dim-witted presiding genius of *The Secret Agent*, whose drawing of a "tangled multitude" of circles suggests "a rendering of cosmic chaos, the symbolism of a mad art attempting the inconceivable" (45), the artist is kin to the creation he renders. "We remain brothers on the lowest side of our intellect and in the instability of our feelings," as Conrad writes in *The Mirror of the Sea* (29), directly attesting to his conviction of the artist's solidarity with the world and the life of unreason that he imagines.

"The word pilot," the omniscient narrator of *The End of the Tether* reflects, awakens "the idea of trust." With his extensive local knowledge and his "certitude of the ship's position," the pilot brings "clear-eyed help" to the seaman "groping blindly in fogs" (250). His sure wisdom allows him to penetrate obscurities with confidence. That position of responsibility is analogous to the role Dare-Devil Harry Whalley imagines himself to occupy relative to humanity at large. The aging pioneer of the China Sea, his name memorialized by an island marked with "a fixed white light" (176), believes that, with enlightened leadership, mankind must inevitably progress. "Somebody must lead the way" (286), Whalley is convinced; and he counts himself among those qualified to assume that charge. A self-appointed member of the illuminati, he acts with the assurance of a moral pilot able confidently to read God's "declared will" in the pages of the Bible (289). Even with the approach of blindness in old age, the master of the *Sofala* is pleased to think of himself as a leader of a humanity advancing "in knowledge of truth, in decency, in justice, in order—in honesty, too, since men harmed each other mostly from ignorance" (288).

The context in which the reflection on the word *pilot* arises defines with mordant irony the inconsequence in Whalley's assumption of authority in matters beyond his competence. It is his native helmsman, not the captain, who brings the word to mind. As Sterne, the disloyal first mate consumed by the ambition to command, puzzles over Whalley's mystifying behavior on the bridge, the inconceivable truth, that the man cannot see, comes to him in a flash of analogical insight: the Serang is to Whalley what a pilot-fish is to a whale (251). *The End of the Tether* not only repeats the terms of Montaigne's analogy in the "Apologie de Raimond Sebond," even to its faulty zoology—sharks not whales, are accompanied by pilot-fish, as Conrad's narrator remarks (250)—but shares its burden as well: a society led by a fool is like a vessel without a rudder and a whale without a pilot-fish. The weak-eyed and unguided whale, according to Montaigne, wanders errantly and swims to its death on a reef (2.12.145). The *Sofala* dies in just that way, and her blind captain with her. Master and ship come to disaster because of the uncertainty ignorance confers. At the critical moment, when he begins to suspect that something is terribly amiss—Massy, with Whalley co-owner of the *Sofala* and her first engineer, has set chunks of soft iron near the compass—the captain freezes in "irresolution," is seized with "the horror of incertitude" (328). Unable to see clearly, Whalley does not know what should or should not be done: "The unusual had come, and he was not fit to deal with it" (328–29). The ignorant man cannot trust himself to answer "Yes or No to a question" (303). Whalley the unknowing, his eyes wandering "irresolutely in space" instead of "going straight to the point, with the assured keen glance of a sailor" (217), shows himself as competent to command as a fool is to assume the role of trustworthy sage.

The absurdity of Whalley's vain posturing follows from his divining of light and certitude where there are only chance and doubt. He is like his partner Massy, once winner of the Manila Lottery, who obsessively compiles lists of numbers in his search for "some logic lurking somewhere in the results of chance." Alone at night, in a smoke-filled room, the gambler not given to reason—"He thought with difficulty and felt vividly"—draws a sure inference from "the incertitude of chance": Massy believes with "unshaken confidence" that he has solved the enigma of the lottery (266–69). A vision of numbers flaming in the night spells out the wondrous solution of the gambler and volatile engineer convinced that he is "fit to be trusted with the whole charge of a ship" (268). The cigar-puffing Dare-Devil Harry Whalley, smoke pouring from his mouth as he speaks words of wisdom regarding the declared will of God and the sure working out of that will in his own contribution to humanity's ordered progress (289), is as acute a logician and sage. In a universe of unreason pictured as "a whirligig of some sort" (263), "a sort of inferno" (269), "a jolly deep hole [. . .] so jolly dark" (306–7) filled with coils of "lines . . . all confused and mingling darkly everywhere" (305) and sulphurous fog which turns the sun "blood-red at midday" (194), Whalley presumes to see the hand of heavenly wisdom plainly writ.

The End of the Tether, then, offers a spectacle of illogic centered on an incompetent sage. Whalley's descent into the blind world of chance is, by analogical extension, an entry into the purely spectacular world of art, which defies lucid ethical reading. And the ironic syntax of the moral relationships staged by Conrad's fiction accords well with his conviction that the artist appeals to the capricious emotions and not to that part of our being which is dependent on wisdom. It is not simply out of illogical presumption that Whalley desperately strives to retain his command by posing as a sighted man. There is also the captain's love for his daughter Ivy at work in the mysterious arrangement of logic leading him to the end of his tether and suicide. Should his deceit be unmasked, he would lose more than his command: he would forfeit his share in the *Sofala,* all the money he has left to bequeath to his poor daughter burdened with an invalid husband, thanks to the sudden and unpredicted collapse of the Travancore & Deccan Banking Corporation. Whalley chooses to go down with his ship, thereby concealing from the authorities the fact of his blindness and tacitly validating Massy's lie to the insurance people in order that Ivy may receive a final gift from her loving father. "Reason was of no use. It was a matter of feeling" (211–12). The foolish sage and the treacherous lover are near allied: each is "a poor devil" (215, 299, 325) who goes "to the devil" (204, 260, 335). Like the artist, the man of folly and feeling dwells in the abyss of infernal regions.

Analogically announced by the union of a brightly lit ivy-covered tower with its upside-down ebony image in the mirror of the sea

(245), love and betrayal join in hellish embrace in the ethically ambiguous *End of the Tether*. As unreasoning as his wisdom is absurd, Whalley's filial love—Ivy "had twined herself tightly round his heart . . . as to a tower of strength" (174)—[25]is instrumental in the unrolling of merciless logic that draws his life down to "the bottom of a precipitous gorge" where "a mass of roots intertwined as if wrestling" (265, 257). Kin to the untrustworthy fool, the man encoiled in the complexities of feeling is fit to serve as a model for the artist, a fellow wrestler in that lonely region where fire and ice unite and where wisdom has no place. "Blessed are all simple emotions, be they dark or bright! It is the lurid intermixture of the two that produces the illuminating blaze of the infernal regions," Melville had underscored in his copy of Hawthorne's "Rappacini's Daughter."[26] What illumination Conrad's tale of life "in a sort of inferno" does provide is of that kind.

This is not to suggest, however, that the ethically indifferent Conradian artist observing the spectacle of human folly has no sympathy for and with his creation. The words of Ivy's reaction to Whalley's letter from the grave—"She read no more that day" (338)—have pathos enough to evoke Francesca da Rimini's tale in the circle of Dante's Hell reserved for those who have subjugated reason to passion. *Quel giorno più non vi leggemmo avante* (5.138) (We read no more of it that day), she recalls of the aftermath of love's victory.[27] And *The End of the Tether* as a whole echoes the words of Francesca's plaint:

> *Nessun maggior dolore,*
> *Che ricordarsi del tempo felice*
> *Nella miseria.*
> (5.121–23).
> [There is no greater pain than, in
> our misery, to be reminded of a
> happy time.][28]

In earlier and prosperous days, Whalley had been able to see and chance had favored him. When one grows infirm or suffers from a fever, as the aging Montaigne repeats the Dantean pathos in his delirium, best to forget the days of health, *che ricordarsi il ben doppia la noia* (for the remembrance of past pleasure doubles the pain) (*Essais* 2.12.160). The author's note to the 1917 edition of the volume including *Youth, Heart of Darkness*, and *The End of the Tether* bespeaks a similar reaction to painful anamnesis, almost wistfully. "A fair half of the book," the sixty-year-old Conrad recalls of *The End of the Tether*, is the product of his experience of the mariner's life: "That experience belongs (like 'Youth's') to the time before I ever thought of putting pen to paper." But when he leaves the time and the world of sighted men and approaches "the veiled region of artistic values," Conrad can only say that he can say nothing. "It would be improper and indeed dangerous" for him to enter that zone of mystery, where no sure guidance is possible and where each reader, tragically, must grope for himself. In words that seem deliberately to echo Ivy's reaction to her father's last words in a "gray twilight" ebbing into night (*The End of the Tether*, 339), Conrad records his own response to the life of ambiguity written in the proofs of his tale: "It is not very likely that I shall ever read 'The End of the Tether' again. No more need be said."[29] Travelers in the region of art can be offered no further guidance by the artist. He is in sympathy with their plight.

Not long after preparing the author's note to the *Youth* volume, Conrad writes in *Notes on Life and Letters* that his "confidence rests on the hearts of men who do not change" and on the sharp-eyed sailor, for whom "the greatest desideratum . . . is to be 'certain of his position'" (208). His confidence does not rest on the indeterminacies of art, where all is doubtful. For Conrad, the artist who postures as a "guide for the practical," in the words of Carlyle,[30] is a treacherous confidence man feeding on humanity's folly. Like skepticism in the guise of knowledge, art advancing itself as wisdom is "blindness laying-down the Law of Optics," as Carlyle's "The Hero as King" (1840) goes on, at its own peril, to say.[31] Conrad agrees with the mind that asks in *Sartor Resartus:* "What counsel to any man, or to any woman" can the writer give, whose thinking jerks "to and fro, in minute incessant fluctuation . . .?"[32] Counsel may indeed by given, by non sequitur, but should never be taken by those who prize wisdom and their lives. Like Montaigne's *Essais*, Conrad's speculative fictions, founded as they are on the unstable emotions and their roundabout logic, contain their own warning. The artist of *The End of the Tether* seconds the notice posted in plain view by the Renaissance skeptic:

> Pour moy, qui me louëroit d'estre bon pilote . . . je ne luy en devrois nul grammercy. . . . On me pourroit tenir pour sage en telle condition de sagesse que je tien pour sottise. (3.5.62)

Art is folly, Conrad agrees, its grammar of unreason "la logique suprême . . . la logique qui mène à la folie," as he reckons in a letter of 1899.[33] Not a knowing seer in a welter of uncertainty, the artist is but another untrustworthy fool in "a community of blind men."[34] If he has any wisdom to convey, it is this: *caveat lector!* He is no pilot.

Postscript: The Consolation of Folly

> But Light is Fire, and Fire is Light;
> And mariners are glad for these,—
> The torch that flares along the coast,
> The star that beams above the seas.
> —Montgomery Schuyler, "Carlyle and Emerson"

> The archaeologist of the future will probably point to this age as a time when the beauty of black was understood.
> —Oscar Wilde, "The Truth of Masks"

> It's a wise person, I guess, who knows he's dumb, and an honest person who knows he's a liar. And it's a dumb person, I guess, who's convinced he's wise, I concluded to myself (wisely). . . . We wander all about, sashay around . . . till we all drop dead.
> —Joseph Heller, *Something Happened*

IN *The Novel and the Modern World* (1939), David Daiches takes Conrad to task for a want of consecutive thinking. While Conrad affirms that the author "must preserve an attitude of perfect indifference,"[1] he also claims for himself as an artist "the faculty of so much insight as can be expressed in a voice of sympathy and compassion."[2] The non sequitur of *Victory,* Daiches alleges, follows from this fundamental contradiction in Conrad's attitude to his characters: it is a "story of virtue untriumphant," which the author "managed to make . . . end on a note of triumph."[3] The Conradian inconsequence in principle and practice argues that "Conrad was no philosopher."[4] Daiches's reasoning is formally elegant; and, certainly, there is sufficient contradiction at work in Conrad's fictional universe to sustain the argument that the teaching of wisdom is not its end.

The inconsequence that Daiches infers, however, does not necessarily follow from the premises he instances. By "perfect indifference," Conrad refers to the artist's disinterestedness, the ethical indifference of the writer striving to render justice to "the intimate alliance of contradictions" (*A Personal Record,* 36) that constitutes a purely spectacular universe. Unlike moralists of the kind Hume holds up to ridicule in *A Treatise of Human Nature*—these deduce *ought* and *ought not* from *is* and *is not*—[5]the artist finds his proper work in seeing and picturing nothing but the truth his fading twilight makes visible. And *how* the Conradian artist sees is by descending within, into the abyssal mirror of the self, there to read as faithfully as he can the underlying truth of a world devoid of reason and ethical purpose. The artist so engaged, then, can reasonably claim to be in lively sympathy with and to have a compassion for the humanity he sees and creates: he shares in the lives he dreams. "The mind of man is capable of anything—because everything is in it," as *Heart of Darkness* (96) rewrites the observation from Montaigne prominently displayed in Pater's *Gaston de Latour:* "every man carries in him the entire form of the human condition."[6] In solidarity with the dreamers he sets in a welter of unreason so dark and confusing as to obscure ethical differences, the artist, too, is "a poor devil" in a universal democracy of the blind (*The End of the Tether*, 215, 299, 325). Conrad, like Montaigne and Melville, squarely faces the logical implications which the artist's participation in that condition of folly has for the object of his own enterprise. *Selon qu'on peut*[7] is the perennial response of the seer who comes to confront his blindness. Not for Conrad the inconsequence and the lectern of the Victorian nightthinkers enlightening the public on love, justice, worship, and the conduct of life.

There is evidence in Daiches's Gifford Lectures of 1983 that the teacher has come round to a way of thinking strikingly similar to Conrad's. Having launched his *God and the Poets* (1984) with a recollection of Hume's coup de grâce to natural theology, Daiches comes to observe in the final lecture, "Poetry and Belief," that indifferent observation and sympathy are not incompatible:

> Perhaps it is the sceptic who is the one capable of the most generous response to poetry of different ages and cultures, the uncommitted openminded eclectic observer of the varieties of human efforts to explain the contradictions and mysteries revealed by human experience. But the sceptic in this sense cannot be the mere observer. He does not stand outside human race but shares the dilemmas of those he responds to.[8]

God and the Poets shows Daiches a skeptic of this kind, a sympathetic observer indifferently poised between the different and conflicting creeds of poets widely separated in time and place. Hogg, Burns, Emily Dickinson, Milton, Whitman, Herbert, Keats, Job, Wallace Stevens, and Dante are but a few of the writers gathered together to celebrate "the achievement of imaginative literature . . . in exploring and illuminating the bafflingly mixed human condition."[9] So mixed is that condition as reflected in Daiches's array of poets and so baffling the variety of creeds they engage or advance, that the substance of poetry, it follows for the disinterested observer, cannot be said to reside in belief or doctrine, nor its purpose in teaching. What illumination, then, can imaginative literature shed on life? The truth of poetry, as Daiches ends *God and the Poets* on a note of affirmation, resides not in its sense, but in "the cadence . . . the incantatory effect" of its music, which consoles and sustains a humanity needy of benediction in a place of turmoil and uncertainty.[10] The lecturer's summation confirms the profession made in his preface: he is "a literary critic and a literary historian, not a philosopher."[11]

The ending of *God and the Poets* recalls the position of the Victorian sage as described by John Holloway in 1953. "He who wants to persuade should put his trust not in the right argument, but in the right word," as Holloway cites from "A Familiar Preface" to *A Personal Record*, in illustration of the Victorian sage's "disparagement of logic" and his adoption of "the essentially individualist methods of the artist."[12] "The power of sound has always been greater than the power of sense," Conrad immediately goes on to explain.[13] Daiches in 1983, Conrad, and Holloway's Victorian sage agree: the artist appeals to the emotions by means of the music of language. Using all the devices that a rhetoric unconstrained by the logic of noncontradiction puts at his disposal, the artist strives to convince the reader of the truth of his feelings.

But Conrad's account of the nature and object of the imagination's enterprise sharply distinguishes the artist's work from the sage's. Ironically enough, his portrait of the artist is consistent with the skeptical Daiches's observation in the sixth of his Gifford Lectures, "Mood Poetry: The Dilemma of Solipsism," that "the doubting or agnostic poet tends to be a brooder."[14] Music, "the art of arts," according to the Preface to *The Nigger of the "Narcissus,"* can console. But the benediction sound confers is the poor consolation of the mind snared in the great privacy of unreason such as Pater had pictured some thirty years before Conrad set to paper his tale of the ship *Narcissus*. The 1868 "Conclusion" to Pater's *The Renaissance* offers this tacit tribute to Montaigne and Hume:

> Experience, already reduced to a group of impressions, is ringed round for each one of us by that thick wall of personality through which no real voice has ever pierced on its way to us. . . . Every one of those impressions is the impression of the individual in his isolation, each mind keeping as a solitary prisoner its own dream of a world.[15]

The words of recollection in *Heart of Darkness*, of a blindfolded somnambulist circling in a nightmare to the rhythm of throbbing drums, describe the consolation sound can bring to the prisoner of such a solipsism, which neither reason nor the language of sense can penetrate: "A steady droning sound of many men chanting each to himself some weird incantation came out of the black, flat wall of the woods . . . and had a strange narcotic effect upon my half-awake senses" (140–41). Senseless babble sings the song of consolation. Music dulls the pain of folly.[16]

Conrad's notion of the artist as a rhetorician of sound parodies the vocation of the Victorian sage striving to awaken his audience from its dogmatic slumber by the inarticulate speech of music. "Wisdom is somehow an opening of the eyes," writes Holloway; and the sage's task, one "of awakening or reawakening something."[17] If that is the Victorian sage's object, the rhetoric of unreason he takes for his means is well designed, not to awaken, but to plunge the reader into a deeper sleep, by numbing the understanding and obscuring the sight. Distinctions fade away in that dark and drowsy state. The sage's work, like the artist's, "comes to possess a non-logical unity," according to Holloway.[18] It has the unity of music, "the type of all the arts" for Wilde, who, with Montaigne, Pater, and the symbolist poets, hears in the sound of its *discordia concors* the syntax of aesthetic reconciliation and ethical indifference: "A Truth in art is that whose contradictory is also true."[19] This is not to say that the Victorian artist as sage provides no service of public and practical value. In the words of Nietzsche's *Ecce Homo*, the musical thinker's "vocation [fills] . . . that need of lulling a feeling of emptiness and hunger, by means of an art which is a narcotic," an "opiate."[20] The sound of the Victorian sage's art produces a narcosis precious to the solitary mind inhabiting a place of folly, endlessly spinning in an abyss of stress and strife and doubt, where extremes meet. He is a bona fide citizen of "a whirling, fire-smote, ice-locked, disease-stricken, space-lost bulb,"[21] as Stephen Crane described the world in the last year of the nineteenth century.

Notes

Preface

1. Eugen Biser, "Wisdom," in *Encyclopedia of Theology: The Concise "Sacramentum Mundi,"* ed. Karl Rahner (New York: Seabury Press, 1975), 1818, 1821.
2. A. L. Le Quesne, *Carlyle* (Oxford: Oxford University Press, 1982), 82–93.
3. James Joyce, "Ibsen's New Drama," *Fortnightly Review* (1900); cited from *The Correspondence of Emerson and Carlyle,* ed. John Slater (New York: Columbia University Press, 1964), 72n.33.
4. Alexandre Micha, in his introduction to Michel de Montaigne's *Essais,* 3 vols. (Paris: Garnier-Flammarion, 1969), 1:27.
5. Stanley Fish, *Self-Consuming Artifacts: The Experience of Seventeenth-Century Literature* (Berkeley: University of California Press, 1972), 3.
6. Walter Kaufmann, *From Shakespeare to Existentialism* (New York: Beacon Press, 1959; reprint, Garden City, N.Y.: Doubleday, 1960), 270.
7. John Sterling, "On the Writings of Carlyle," in his *Essays and Tales,* ed. Julius Charles Hare, 2 vols. (London: W. H. Parker, 1848), 1:279–80.

Introduction: The Victorian *Fol Sage*

1. Harold Bloom, *Figures of Capable Imagination* (New York: Seabury Press, 1976), 43.
2. Ibid., 43.
3. Walter E. Houghton, *The Victorian Frame of Mind, 1830–1870* (New Haven: Yale University Press, 1957), 15, 17.
4. Walter Pater, *Plato and Platonism* (New York and London: Macmillan & Co., 1893), 174.
5. Bloom, *Figures,* 45.
6. John Holloway, *The Victorian Sage: Studies in Argument* (London: Macmillan, 1953), 1, 293.
7. Ibid.
8. See Robert Shackleton, *Montesquieu: A Critical Biography* (Oxford: Oxford University Press, 1961), 252.
9. John Sterling, "Montaigne and His Writings," *London and Westminster Review* 29 (August 1838): 321–52. The article was prompted by the announcement of Sir Frederick Madden's discovery, in 1837, of a copy of Florio's Montaigne autographed by Shakespeare. Emerson, in 1848, and Melville, in 1849, examined the copy at the British Museum.

10. Charles-Augustin Sainte-Beuve, *Port-Royal,* ed. René Louis Doyon and Charles Marchesné (Paris: La Connaissance, 1926), 3:13, 59–60.
11. Charles Dédéyan, *Montaigne chez ses amis anglo-saxons: Montaigne dans le romantisme anglais et ses prolongements victoriens,* 2 vols. (Paris: Boivin, 1943).
12. Holloway, *Victorian Sage,* 3, 297.
13. Bloom, *Figures,* 45.
14. Holloway, *Victorian Sage,* 6, 290, 296.
15. Ibid., 10, 296.
16. Cited in ibid., 10.
17. Ibid., 4.
18. Cited in ibid., 16.
19. *The Nigger of the "Narcissus":* "Haven't we, together and upon the immortal sea, wrung out a meaning from our sinful lives? Goodbye, brothers! You were a good crowd. . . ." *Sartor Resartus:* "Fare-*well*! Have we not, in the course of Eternity, travelled some months in our Life-journey in partial sight of one another; have we not existed together, though in a state of quarrel." See Joseph Conrad, *Youth, Heart of Darkness, and The End of the Tether* (London: J. M. Dent, 1946–55), 7 (all subsequent references to Conrad's works are taken from the Dent's Collected Edition).
20. See Camille R. La Bossière, *Joseph Conrad and the Science of Unknowing* (Fredericton, N.B.: York Press, 1979), 20.
21. Cited in Holloway, *Victorian Sage,* 4.
22. Thomas Carlyle, *Sartor Resartus and On Heroes and Hero Worship,* with an introd. by W. H. Hudson (London: J. M. Dent, 1908), 292.
23. Carlyle, *On Heroes,* 279, 295.
24. Eloise Knapp Hay, "Impressionism Limited," in *Joseph Conrad: A Commemoration,* ed. Norman Sherry (London: Macmillan, 1976), 61. This point is taken up by Ian Watt's *Conrad in the Nineteenth Century* (Berkeley: University of California Press, 1979), 171.
25. Conrad, *Lord Jim,* 4.
26. Conrad, *Heart of Darkness,* 77.
27. Michel de Montaigne, *Essais,* ed. and with an introd. by Alexandre Micha, 3 vols. (Paris: Garnier-Flammarion, 1969), 3.2.21.
28. Richard William Church, *The Essays of Montaigne* (London: J. W. Parker & Son, 1857), 247, 251.
29. Montaigne, 1.23.168.
30. Ibid., 2.2.12.
31. Ibid., 3.13.300.

Chapter 1. Carlyle and Montaigne: Their Silent Conversation

1. *The Correspondence of Emerson and Carlyle,* edited and with an introduction by Joseph Slater (New York and London: Columbia University Press, 1964), 197.
2. John Sterling, "Montaigne and His Writings," *London and Westminster Review* 29 (August 1838): 321–52.
3. Kenneth Marc Harris, *Carlyle and Emerson: Their Long Debate* (Cambridge: Harvard University Press, 1978), 83.
4. Henry James, Jr., "The Correspondence of Carlyle and Emerson," *Century Magazine* 26 (June 1883): 269.

5. Ralph L. Rusk, *The Life of Ralph Waldo Emerson* (New York and London: Columbia University Press, 1949), 195.

6. Slater, *Correspondence*, 88.

7. A. Abbott Ikeler, *Puritan Temper and Transcendental Faith: Carlyle's Literary Vision* (Columbus: Ohio State University Press, 1972), 211.

8. Slater, *Correspondence*, 193.

9. Ibid., 44.

10. Charles Dédéyan, *Montaigne chez ses amis anglo-saxons: Montaigne dans le romantisme anglais et ses prolongements victoriens*, 2 vols. (Paris: Boivin, 1943), 1:155–56.

11. Ibid., 1:154.

12. Slater, *Correspondence*, 459, 460.

13. Rusk, *Emerson*, 377.

14. Thomas Carlyle, *Sartor Resartus and On Heroes and Hero Worship*, with an introd. by W. H. Hudson (London: J. M. Dent, 1908), 38, 1, 51 (all subsequent references are to this edition).

15. The figure is borrowed from Harris (*Carlyle and Emerson*, 2), who borrows it from *Sartor Resartus* (22).

16. Michel de Montaigne, *Essais*, ed. and with an introd. by Alexandre Micha, 3 vols. (Paris: Garnier-Flammarion, 1969), 2.12.112 (all subsequent references are to this edition).

17. Charles-Augustin Sainte-Beuve, *Port-Royal*, ed. René Louis Doyon and Charles Marchesné (Paris: La Connaissance, 1926), 3:36.

18. Cited from Etienne Gilson, *Reason and Revelation in the Middle Ages* (New York: Charles Scribner's Sons, 1938), 93.

19. Kate Wilhelm, "The Fusion Bomb," in *The Infinity Box* (New York: Harper & Row, 1977), 201.

20. Ralph Waldo Emerson, *The Complete Works*, ed. Edward Waldo Emerson, 12 vols. Centenary Edition (Boston and New York: Houghton Mifflin Co., 1903–4), 4:156, 182. See also, *The Journals and Miscellaneous Notebooks of Ralph Waldo Emerson*, ed. William Gilman et al. (Cambridge: Belknap Press of Harvard University, 1960–), 11:116. "Wer nicht liebt Wein, Weib, und Gesang, / Der bleibt ein Narr, sein Leben lang," copied by Emerson in the Luther Room of Wartburg Castle, is used in "Montaigne; or, The Sceptic."

21. Alfred Glauser, *Montaigne paradoxal* (Paris: A. G. Nizet, 1972), 9.

22. *Les Pages immortelles de Montaigne*, ed., selected, and with an introd. by André Gide (Paris and New York: Editions Corrêa and Longmans Green, 1939), 37–38. So great is the charm of unreason for Gide, that he finds even the "Apologie de Raimond Sebond" too lucid and purposeful in design to suit his artist's taste.

23. John O'Neill, *Essaying Montaigne: A Study of the Renaissance Institution of Writing and Reading* (London: Routledge & Kegan Paul, 1982), 127. In accordance with Stanley Fish's reading of seventeenth-century "self-consuming artifacts," O'Neill finds pedagogical and ethical virtue in Montaigne's play of paradoxy: it shows that "genuine knowledge is always relative to one's nature" (190).

24. Réjean Ducharme, *Les Enfantômes* (Paris: Gallimard, 1976), 94.

25. See Blaise Pascal, *Pensées*, ed. and with an introd. by Léon Brunschigg (Paris: Le Livre de Poche, 1972), 163: "La fièvre a ses frissons et ses ardeurs; et le froid montre aussi bien la grandeur de l'ardeur de la fièvre que le chaud même."

26. Glauser, *Montaigne paradoxal*, 51–55.

27. Henri Brémond, *La Poésie pure* (Paris: Grasset, 1926), 119–23.

28. See Otilio Lopez Fanego, "Quelques précisions sur Montaigne et l'inquisition espagnole," in *Montaigne et les Essais, 1580–1980*, ed. François Moreau, Robert

Granderoute, and Claude Blum (Paris and Geneva: Champion & Slatkine, 1983), 369. Edward FitzGerald, the translator of *Six Dramas of Calderón* (1853), was among the Victorian students of European literature to compare the *Essais* with *Life Is a Dream*, as Dédéyan points out (*Montaigne chez ses amis*, 1:367–68).

29. Camille R. La Bossière, *Joseph Conrad and the Science of Unknowing* (Fredericton, N.B.: York Press, 1979), 15.

30. Robert Ter Horst, *Calderón: The Secular Plays* (Lexington: University of Kentucky Press, 1982), 89–90.

31. Ibid., 97, 232. Ter Horst concludes his study with a comparison of the "philosophy" of *Life Is a Dream* with Hume's in the *Enquiry concerning Human Understanding*.

32. Arthur Schopenhauer, *The World as Will and Idea*, trans. R. B. Haldane, 3 vols. (London: Routledge & Kegan Paul, 1883–86), 1:22, 62, 463–65.

33. Ter Horst, *Calderón*, 24; and Peter Burke, *Montaigne* (Oxford: Oxford University Press, 1981), 15–17.

34. Edmond Vanteenberghe, *Le Cardinal Nicholas de Cues* (Paris: Minerve, 1920), 272–90.

35. Jackson I. Cope, *The Theater and the Dream* (Baltimore: Johns Hopkins University Press, 1973), chaps. 1, 7–8. Cope begins with Cusa's perspectivism and ends with *Life Is a Dream*.

36. Jean Rousset, *Circé et le paon: la littérature de l'âge baroque en France* (Paris: José Corti, 1954), 27.

37. Dédéyan, *Montaigne chez ses amis*, 1:29.

38. See, for example, Richard H. Popkin's introduction to his edition of Hume's *'Dialogues concerning Natural Religion' and the Posthumous Essays, 'Of the Immortality of the Soul' and 'Of Suicide'* (Indianapolis: Hackett Books, 1980), xv.

39. W. H. Alexander, "Johann Georg Hamann," in *The Encyclopedia of Philosophy*, ed. Paul Edwards (New York and London: Collier Macmillan, 1967), 3:407; and Albert Béguin, *L'Ame romantique et le rêve* (Paris: José Corti, 1939), 51–53.

40. Schopenhauer, *World as Will and Idea*, 3:393–94. Schopenhauer distances himself from Hamann and Kant here, by finding in Hume an argument, not for fideism, but for "the untenableness of all optimism."

41. See, for example, Etienne Gilson, *History of Christian Philosophy in the Middle Ages* (New York: Random House, 1955), 536; and J.-Roger Charbonnel, *La Pensée italienne au XVIe siècle et le courant libertin* (Paris: E. Champion, 1919; reprint, Geneva: Slatkine, 1969), 705–7.

42. Alexander, "Hamann," in *Encyclopedia of Philosophy*, 3:406.

43. Wylie Sypher, "The Late-Baroque," in *Four Stages of Renaissance Style* (New York: Doubleday & Co., 1955), 294.

44. Everett W. Hesse, *Calderón de la Barca* (Boston: Twayne, 1967), 99–102; Arturo Farinelli, *La vita è un sogno* (Torino: Fratelli Bocca, 1916), 2:340–43; and Alexander Parker, *The Allegorical Drama of Calderón* (Oxford: Dolphin Press, 1968), 37.

45. A. del Rio, *Historia de la literatura española* (New York: Dryden Press, 1948), 1:329.

46. Henry W. Sullivan, *Calderón in the German lands and the Low Countries: His Reception and Influence, 1654–1980* (Cambridge: Cambridge University Press, 1983), 243.

47. Samuel Taylor Coleridge, *Biographia Literaria*, ed. John Shawcross (Oxford: Clarendon Press, 1907), 1.14.12.

48. Nicholas of Cusa, *Of Learned Ignorance*, trans. G. Heron (London: Routledge & Kegan Paul, 1954), 2:12.

49. By coincidence, "conceptual music" describes Calderón's art for Ter Horst (*Calderón*, 36).
50. Emerson, "Poetry and Imagination," in *Letters and Social Aims: Complete Works*, 8:49–50; and *Journals and Miscellaneous Notebooks*, 11:134.
51. Emerson, "Beauty," in *Nature* (1836), *Complete Works*, 1:18.
52. Thomas Carlyle, "Montaigne," in *Critical and Miscellaneous Essays* (London: Chapman & Hall, 1899), 5:66.
53. Emerson, *Journals and Miscellaneous Notebooks*, 16:222.
54. Ibid., 6:21.
55. Cited from the "Testimonies of Authors" appended to the Dent Edition (1908) of *Sartor Resartus*, 227.
56. Ibid., 230.
57. Michel Butor, *Essais sur les Essais* (Paris: Gallimard, 1968), 71. The rapprochement of poetry and *essai* in the erudite Montaigne is analogous to the reduction of the distance between fiction and *essai* in Butor. "Michel Butor is prepared to write a novel that looks like a short encyclopaedia," Anthony Burgess remarks in *The Novel Now* (London: Faber & Faber, 1967), 16.
58. Butor, *Essais*, 71.
59. Glauser, *Montaigne paradoxal*, 152.
60. Joseph Conrad, *Lord Jim*, 210–14.
61. Joseph Conrad, *A Personal Record*, 36.
62. Joseph Conrad, *Nostromo*, 85.
63. Ralph Waldo Emerson, *Letters*, ed. Ralph L. Rusk (New York: Columbia University Press, 1939), 4:31.
64. Jerry A. Dibble, *The Pythia's Drunken Song: Carlyle's "Sartor Resartus" and the Style Problem in German Idealist Philosophy* (The Hague: Martinus Nijhoff, 1978), 56.
65. Emerson, "Montaigne; or, The Sceptic," in *Representative Men, Collected Works*, 4:149.
66. See S. N. Hampshire, "Hume's Place in Philosophy," in *David Hume: A Symposium*, ed. D. F. Pears (London: Macmillan, 1963), 10. For Hampshire, Hume is more stylist and rhetorician than philosopher: "He aimed . . . at the virtues of the essayist" (3).
67. Barbara Seward, *The Symbolic Rose* (New York: Columbia University Press, 1960), 3.
68. Kenneth Burke, *Language as Symbolic Action* (Berkeley: University of California Press, 1968), 475.
69. Ibid., 475. See, also, Burke's *A Rhetoric of Motives* (Berkeley: University of California Press, 1969), 120: the EVERLASTING YEA, like the "Symbol" an act of "Love," is "Enigmatic."
70. William Blake, *The Portable Blake*, ed. Alfred Kazin (New York: Viking Press, 1968), 594.
71. Joseph Conrad, *Tales of Hearsay*, 1.
72. Ikeler, *Puritan Temper*, 24, 16. At every stage in his career as writer, Carlyle "displays a consistent ambivalence toward art."
73. Slater, *Correspondence*, 130.
74. From his introduction to the 1908 Dent Edition of *Sartor Resartus*, viii.
75. Harris, *Carlyle and Emerson*, 31.
76. Henri-Frédéric Amiel, *Fragments d'un journal intime* (Geneva: H. Georg, 1893), 6th ed., 2:340.
77. Ibid., 2:200. Amiel likens his own dream-thinking to Montaigne's in a journal entry of 1873, the year of the final meeting of Carlyle and Emerson.

78. Oscar Wilde, "The Critic as Artist," in *The Artist as Critic*, ed. Richard Ellmann (New York: Random House, 1969; reprint, Chicago: University of Chicago Press, 1982), 432.
79. Thomas Carlyle, "Essay on Goethe," in *Works*, ed. H. D. Traill (London: Chapman & Hall, 1896–99), 26:405.
80. Glauser, *Montaigne paradoxal*, 42.
81. Pascal, *Pensées*, 177.
82. Joseph Conrad, *Under Western Eyes*, 33.
83. Carlyle, "Montaigne," in *Critical and Miscellaneous Essays*, 5:68–69.
84. Dugald Stewart, "Michel de Montaigne," in *Encyclopaedia Britannica* (1824); cited from Dédéyan, *Montaigne chez ses amis*, vol. 2, appendix 6.
85. See, for example, Murray Baumgarten, "Parameters of Debate: A Reading of Carlyle's Annotations of Mill's *Principles of Political Economy*," in *Carlyle: Books & Margins* (Santa Cruz: University Library of the University of California, 1980). Carlyle's debate with Mill shows him railing against "his own confusions" (126). Evidence of self-contradiction in Carlyle is abundant. His minatory criticism of Zacharias Werner's *The Sons of the Valley* in 1828 as "an inane fever-dream," a formless, boundless phantasmagoria, and his praise, in the same year, of Goethe's *Helena* for being just such a work, is but one of the many additional instances of Carlylean unreason which might be adduced (*Works*, 26:112–13).
86. Carlyle, "Montaigne," in *Critical and Miscellaneous Essays*, 5:66.
87. John Sterling, *Essays and Tales*, ed. Julius Charles Hare (London: W. H. Parker, 1848), 1:374–91.
88. See André Espiau de la Maestre, *Humanisme classique et syncrétisme mythique chez Paul Claudel* (Paris: Honoré Champion, 1977), 278.
89. Conrad, *Under Western Eyes*, 318, 268, 105–6.
90. Slater, *Correspondence*, 98–99.

Chapter 2. Emerson's Divine Comedy

1. As reported by Edward Everett Hale, in an address of May 1893; cited from the introduction to *The Correspondence of Emerson and Carlyle*, ed. John Slater, 43. See Rusk, *The Life of Ralph Waldo Emerson*, 357.
2. *The Journals and Miscellaneous Notebooks of Ralph Waldo Emerson*, ed. W. H. Gilman et. al. (Cambridge: Belknap Press of Harvard University, 1960–), 10:11 (hereafter abbreviated *JMN* and cited in the text).
3. Emerson's words are cited in Ikeler's demonstration of the "circular absurdity" of Carlyle's argument in "The Hero as Poet" (*Puritan Temper*, 24).
4. Sterling, *Essays and Tales*, 1:307. On 14 April 1848, Emerson acknowledged receipt of the two-volume edition of Sterling's works (*The Letters of Ralph Waldo Emerson*, ed. Ralph L. Rusk, 6 vols. [New York and London: Columbia University Press, 1939], 4:53; hereafter abbreviated *L* and cited in the text).
5. Slater, *Correspondence*, 99. And yet, according to Emerson in a letter of 23 January 1835 to Benjamin Peter Hunt, Coleridge's death leaves Carlyle "the best thinker of the age" (*Letters*, 1:432).
6. For a reading at odds with this account of the substance of Clough's comment, see A. L. Le Quesne, *Carlyle* (Oxford: Oxford University Press, 1982), 82–93 in particular. Le Quesne proposes that Carlyle forfeited his role as prophet and leader by his increasing emphasis on the essential role of the hero and by abandoning the "double vision" of the artist to preach from "a single point of view." Had Carlyle

continued in the way of *Sartor Resartus,* holding opposites "in balance," seeing them "simultaneously and with equal vividness," and had he "demanded" democracy of his disciples and not the single-minded politics of heroism, they would have obeyed and continued as faithful followers. Emerson is not mentioned as the recipient of Clough's complaint.

7. *The Complete Works of Ralph Waldo Emerson,* ed. Edward Waldo Emerson, 12 vols., Centenary Edition (Boston and New York: Houghton Mifflin Co., 1903–4), 1:52 (hereafter abbreviated W and cited in the text).

8. Harris, *Carlyle and Emerson,* 68.

9. See, e.g., Leonard Neufeldt, *The House of Emerson* (Lincoln and London: University of Nebraska Press, 1982), 241.

10. See, e.g., B. L. Packer, *Emerson's Fall* (New York: Continuum, 1982), 26.

11. From an anonymous review of *The Conduct of Life,* in the *Southern Literary Messenger* 32 (April 1861); cited from *Critical Essays on Ralph Waldo Emerson,* ed. Robert E. Burkholder and Joel Myerson (Boston: G. K. Hall, 1983), 176.

12. *Poems of R. W. Emerson and O. W. Holmes,* with a biographical introduction by Henry Ketcham (New York and London: Co-operative Publishing Co., 1887), vi. For Charles Pearse Cranch in 1883, Emerson is "the great ethical teacher of the age" ("Ralph Waldo Emerson," *Unitarian Review and Religious Magazine* 20 [July 1883]; cited from Burkholder and Myerson, *Critical Essays,* 209). Howard Mumford Jones concurs in his introduction to *Emerson on Education: Selections* (New York: Teachers' College Press of Columbia University, 1966), 4. Emerson devoted his entire life to the public teaching of moral truth, though what that truth was Jones cannot begin to say: "Emerson could not take a stand on any question without also taking the opposite stand" (13). According to Jones, Emerson's writings rival Blake's prophetic books in obscurity. By contrast, Josephine Miles's *Ralph Waldo Emerson* (Minneapolis: University of Minnesota Press, 1964), distributed to high schools in the United States by the Webster Division of McGraw-Hill, finds that "the aphoristic Jonson of *Timber* is Emerson's direct model" for the writing of wise sayings (33–34). Miles focuses on *The Conduct of Life,* stressing its lucidity, coherence, and practicality. For a concise statement of Emerson's status as a moral authority in his own time and in the years immediately following his death, see Vivian C. Hopkins, *Spires of Form: A Study of Emerson's Aesthetic Theory* (New York: Russell & Russell, 1965), 5.

13. Wilde, *Artist as Critic,* 292.

14. Ibid., 304.

15. Dorothy M. Richardson, *Pilgrimage (IV)* (London: Virago, 1979), 419. Emerson, having authored two books and having taught that "the man who aims to speak as books enable . . . babbles. Let him hush" (W 1:135), reminded himself in 1842: "Cease talking with bellowing emphasis against words" (*JMN* 8:252).

16. Cited from Harris, *Carlyle and Emerson,* 62.

17. Jay Leyda, *The Melville Log: A Documentary Life of Herman Melville, 1819–1891* (New York: Harcourt, Brace, 1951), 2:715.

18. See Rusk's note on Gustav d'Eichtal, *Letters,* 1:374.

19. Cited from Lewis Leary, *Ralph Waldo Emerson: An Interpretive Essay* (Boston: Twayne, 1980), 4. Emerson wrote to Carlyle on 5 August 1850: "We are all in one boat. . . . We are beleaguered with contradictions, and the moment we preach . . . things turn on their heel and leave us to fret alone" (*Letters,* 4:223). Like Carlyle, Emerson beleaguered himself with contradictions.

20. From a letter of November 1838 to his brother William, describing his difficulties in finding a direction for his upcoming "Human Life" course of lectures. See also, *JMN* 2:118, *L* 4:54; *JMN* 9:414, 11:89; and *The Early Lectures of Ralph*

Waldo Emerson, ed. Stephen W. Whicher, Robert E. Spiller, and Wallace E. Williams, 3 vols. (Cambridge: Harvard University Press, 1959–72), 2:358 (hereafter abbreviated *EL* and cited in the text).

21. *The Essential Plotinus: Representative Treatises from the "Enneads*,*"* trans. and with an introd. by Elmer O'Brien (New York: New American Library, 1964), 62. "Contraries necessarily change into each other," "Change is repose," and "The way up and down is one and the same" are the sayings that Plotinus objects to, "dismissing Heraclitus for the moment with words that some may feel excellently applicable to himself," as O'Brien remarks (59). Emerson frequently turned on himself in a similar way. His criticism of American culture for failing to promote high standards of logic and learning (*JMN* 8:121); of Washington politicians for confounding heaviness with lightness, good with evil (*JMN* 10:29); of preachers for their "vasty notion of poetry" and "straining to say what is unutterable" (*JMN* 3:12); of some religions for teaching that man can know nothing (*W* 6:207); of Charles K. Newcomb, a follower of Montaigne, for being "a perverse son of the light fighting against light" (*L* 4:516); of William Ellery Channing for ethical neutrality (*JMN* 9:445); of the American people for forgetting history and not sticking to what they say (*JMN* 11:411); of Amos Bronson Alcott for confounding the vocations of prophet and lecturer (*L* 2:139–41); of the Methodists for preaching against learning, then supporting institutions of higher learning (*L* 3:295); of F. H. Hedge for capricious and circular reasoning (*JMN* 8:31); of Thoreau for his "unlimited contradiction" in praising snow for its warmth (*JMN* 9:9); and of Daniel Webster for adopting one position, then affirming its opposite (*JMN* 11:346–58, 15:76)—these are but a few of the many additional instances of Emersonian self-analysis.

22. Henry Demarest Lloyd, "Emerson's Wit and Humor," *Forum* 22 (December 1896); cited from Burkholder and Myerson, *Critical Essays*, 253, 250.

23. Slater, *Correspondence*, 88.

24. Ibid., 98.

25. Ibid., 144.

26. James Russell Lowell, *A Fable for Critics* (1848); cited from Burkholder and Myerson, *Critical Essays*, 131.

27. Albert Gelpi, "Emerson: The Paradox of Organic Form," in *Emerson: Prophecy, Metamorphosis, and Influence*, ed. David Levin (New York: Columbia University Press, 1975), 169.

28. Ronald Bush, "T. S. Eliot: Singing the Emerson Blues," in *Emerson: Prospect and Retrospect*, ed. Joel Porte (Cambridge: Harvard University Press, 1982), 180.

29. See Harris (107), for a Carlylean reading of Emerson's cheery response to "the utter negation and contradiction of his theories."

30. For an account of Emerson's use of chaos as an architectural principle, see Neufeldt's *The House of Emerson*.

31. David Levin, *Prophecy*, v. See Merton M. Sealts, Jr., "Emerson as Teacher," the final piece in *Emerson Centenary Essays*, ed. Joel Myerson (Carbondale: Southern Illinois University Press, 1982), for a celebration of Emerson as something of an ideal university professor; and Ronald Sukenick, "Art and the Underground," in *American Book Review* 6 (January–February 1984): 2–3, for a recommendation of Emerson as a formal model on which to base the integration of "the pragmatic and the prophetic" in American life and art. Like their subject when he speaks in the prophetic mode, Sealts and Sukenick seem altogether in earnest. The comic spirit, impelled by reason (i.e., the understanding), is no friend to the Emersonian teacher of high moral seriousness. For Emerson on 19 July 1837, laughter is "a disagreeable phenomenon" (*JMN* 5:343).

32. See Edward Waldo Emerson's "Notes" on *Letters and Social Aims* (*W* 8:335).

33. From a letter of October 1833, to his brother John; cited from Ikeler, *Puritan Temper*, 29.

34. Ikeler remarks of Carlyle's criticism of Goethe: "Goethe and his kind . . . appear . . . as misdirected leaders with their feet planted, if not in Hell, at least in a purgatory of moral uselessness" (29).

35. Leyda, *ML* 2:715.

36. Ralph Waldo Emerson, *Young Emerson Speaks: Unpublished Discourses on Many Subjects,* ed. Arthur Cushman McGiffert, Jr. (Boston: Houghton Mifflin Co., 1938), 101 (hereafter abbreviated *YES* and cited in the text).

37. *Parnassus,* ed. Ralph Waldo Emerson (Boston: Houghton, Mifflin & Co., 1874; reprint, Freeport, N.Y.: Books for Libraries Press, 1970), vi.

38. Sherman Paul, *Emerson's Angles of Vision* (Cambridge: Harvard University Press, 1952), 219. See George Henry Calvert, "Ralph Waldo Emerson," *New York Quarterly* 1 (January 1853): "Surrender yourself . . . to his dominion. He will not lead you, like Dante, through Purgatory and Hell, but into calm Elysian Fields of contemplation" (cited from Burkholder and Myers, *Critical Essays,* 161).

39. Gerald Morgan, "Harlequin Faustus: Marlowe's Comedy of Hell," *Humanities Association Bulletin* 18 (1967): 27. The Wittenberg Doctor of Divinity, whose skill in logic we are asked to accept on faith—he has "with concise syllogisms / Gravelled the pastors of the German church," so we are told (1.1.110–11)—is actually a clown wonderfully adept in unreason, turning logic on its head and confounding opposites, as when he conflates Aristotle's *Analytics* with Pierre de la Ramée's *Animadversiones Aristotelicae.* Joel Porte writes of the "strenuous ideal of Faustian expansion" in Emerson, his hunger to reconcile all differences and oppositions in himself (*Representative Man: Ralph Waldo Emerson in His Time,* xi).

40. See, for example, *YES* 102; *JMN* 2:340, 6:143; *EL* 2:153; and *W* 2:109.

41. Michel de Montaigne, *Essais,* ed. and with an introd. by Alexandre Micha, 3 vols. (Paris: Garnier-Flammarion, 1969), 3.11.246 (all subsequent references are to this edition).

42. *Essays of Michel de Montaigne,* trans. by Charles Cotton, and selected and illus. by Salvador Dali (Garden City, N.Y.: Doubleday & Co., 1947). The illustration, inscribed *Fortis Imaginatio Generat Casum,* follows page 408. See Réginald Dalle, "Montaigne vu par Salvador Dali," in *Montaigne et les Essais,* ed. Moreau, Granderoute, and Blum, 346. Dalle considers the proximity of Montaigne's humanism to Dali's surrealism.

43. Rousset, *Circé et le paon,* 27, 140–41.

44. See above, n.21.

45. Gide, in his introduction to *Les Pages immortelles de Montaigne,* 38.

46. From Blake's "Notes on the Illustrations to Dante," in *The Portable Blake,* ed. Kazin, 594.

47. In "De la praesumption," Montaigne writes that liars are trustworthy when they predict a heat wave at Christmas (2.17.318). His knowledge of parts of the world below the equator suggests an extension of the joke—and one in accord with the spirit of Emerson here.

48. "Extremes meet" is the first of the introductory aphorisms in Coleridge's *Aids to Reflection* (1825), a work well known to Emerson. The illustration of the aphorism with "cold performs th'effect of fire" is recorded in *The Notebooks of Samuel Taylor Coleridge,* ed. Kathleen Coburn (London: Routledge, 1957), 1:item 1725. In *The Friend,* Coleridge writes: "Extremes meet—a proverb . . . to collect and explain all the instances and exemplifications of which, would constitute and exhaust all philosophy" (*The Collected Works,* ed. Barbara Rooke [London: Routledge & Kegan Paul, 1969], 4:110).

Notes 111

49. See also, *W* 7:181, 8:313, 9:14; *JMN* 4:383, 7:162, 12:400, 14:338, 16:89.

50. In Hebrew, Uriel signifies "Fire of God." The fact that, in medieval Judaism, he served as an emblem of the heat of day during winter and that, in Gnosticism, he was sometimes represented by a snake, may have played some part in Emerson's choice of him as a spokesman for "Extremes meet."

51. Coleridge uses the Ouroboros in a similar way, as an emblem for poetry's wholeness. See *Collected Letters of Samuel Taylor Coleridge*, ed. E. L. Griggs (Oxford: Clarendon Press, 1959), 4:545–46: "The common end of . . . *all* Poems is to convert a *series* into a *Whole:* to make those events, which in real or imagined History move on in a *strait* line, assume to our Understanding a *circular* motion—the snake with it's Tail in its Mouth." The letter, dated 7 March 1815, is to Joseph Cottle.

52. Emerson copied these words from Friedrich Ast's *Platons Leben und Schriften* (1816), according to the editor's note for this entry.

53. Friedrich Nietzsche, *Thus Spoke Zarathustra*, trans. and with an introd. by R. J. Hollingdale (Harmondsworth: Penguin Books, 1961), 330. Much of "The Intoxicated Song," first published in the early 1890s, reads like a translation of Emerson. For example: "All joy wants the eternity of all things, wants honey, wants dregs, wants intoxicated midnight, wants graves, wants the consolation of graveside tears, wants gilded sunsets . . . *what* does joy not want! it is thirstier, hungrier . . . than all woe, it wants *itself;* it bites into itself . . ." (332). For Zarathustra as for Emerson, "midnight is also noonday" (330).

54. Howard Nemerov, "Glass Dialectic," in *The Image and the Law* (1947); cited from *The Collected Poems of Howard Nemerov* (Chicago: University of Chicago Press, 1977), 30. See also, Nemerov's *Journal of the Fictive Life* (Chicago: University of Chicago Press, 1965), 155, 182: since all art, like poetry, is a dreaming, a gazing into a mirror, it is strictly autotelic and of no practical use.

55. Elizabeth Palmer Peabody, "Nature—A Prose Poem," *United States Magazine, and Democratic Review* 1 (February 1838); cited from Burkholder and Myerson, *Critical Essays*, 31, 28.

56. George Santayana, "Ralph Waldo Emerson," in *American Prose: Selections with Critical Introductions by Various Writers*, ed. George Rice Carpenter (New York: Macmillan, 1898); cited from Burkholder and Myerson, *Critical Essays*, 259–60. It is difficult not to suspect mischief in the philosopher's reading.

57. Leary, *Emerson*, 59, 124. "At best, he fumbles toward what cannot be expressed," Leary also remarks of Emerson's thought (65). See Jerome Loving, *Emerson, Whitman, and the American Muse* (Chapel Hill: University of North Carolina Press, 1982), 123: Emerson is often "intentionally vague at critical junctures . . . to allow his audience to fill in the answers." For Gayle L. Smith, Emerson's " 'imperfect' sentences do demand new activity on our part" ("Reading Emerson on the Right Side of the Brain," *Modern Language Studies* 15 [1985]: 31).

58. Porte, *Representative Man*, xi.

59. Stanley Rosen, *Nihilism: A Philosophical Essay* (New Haven: Yale University Press, 1969), 277.

60. This passage, entered in Emerson's journal in September 1842, is altered slightly for "Experience," in *Essays: Second Series* (*W* 3:80). Cats and their tails seem to have held a certain fascination for Emerson. On one occasion, he likened the feline tail to a snake: they are a "beautiful horror" (*JMN* 11:42).

61. Joseph F. Doherty, "Emerson and the Loneliness of the Gods," *Texas Studies in Literature and Language* 16 (Spring 1974); cited from Burkholder and Myerson, *Critical Essays*, 433.

62. Robert E. Burkholder, "The Contemporary Reception of *English Traits*," in *Emerson Centenary Essays*, ed. Myerson, 172.

63. Sanford E. Marovitz, "Emerson's Shakespeare: From Scorn to Apotheosis," in *Emerson Centenary Essays,* ed. Myerson, 153, 155.

64. Glauser, *Montaigne paradoxal,* 152. On the same page, Glauser remarks of Montaigne's work: "Elle s'engendre et se nourrit d'elle-même."

65. Dr. John Carlyle consulted this edition in preparing his translation of the *Inferno.*

66. The figure of Tantalus reaching out for one thing to find it converted to its opposite is borrowed from Ter Horst, *Calderón* (170).

Chapter 3. Melville's Mute Glass

1. Jay Leyda, *The Melville Log: A Documentary Life of Herman Melville (1819–1891),* 2 vols. (New York: Harcourt, Brace, 1951), 2:793–94 (hereafter abbreviated *ML* and cited in the text).

2. Preface to *New Perspectives on Melville,* ed. Faith Pullin (Kent, Ohio and Edinburgh: Kent State University Press and Edinburgh University Press, 1978), x–xi; and the introduction to *Melville,* ed. Richard Chase (Englewood Cliffs, N.J.: Prentice-Hall, 1962), 3.

3. See Tom Quirk, *Melville's Confidence Man: From Knave to Knight* (Columbia: University of Missouri Press, 1982), 58–73.

4. Herman Melville, "Hawthorne and His Mosses," in *Billy Budd and Other Prose Pieces* (New York: Russell & Russell, 1963), 131. Melville's works, with the exception of *The Confidence-Man,* are cited from this, the Standard Edition, in 16 volumes.

5. Melville, "Art," in *Poems,* 270.

6. Sir Thomas Browne, *Religio Medici,* in *The Consolation of Philosophy,* ed. Irwin Edman (New York: Modern Library, 1943), 389.

7. Herman Melville, *The Confidence-Man: His Masquerade,* ed. Hershel Parker (New York: W. W. Norton & Co., 1971), 209 (all subsequent references are to this edition).

8. See *The Confidence-Man,* 206, n.1.

9. Gerhard von Rad, *Wisdom in Israel,* trans. James D. Martin (London: SCM, 1972), 250. Glendon A. Bryce, on the other hand, finds that wisdom literature possessed a "note of agnosticism" from the beginning (*A Legacy of Wisdom: The Egyptian Contribution to the Wisdom of Israel* [Lewisburg: Bucknell University Press, 1979], 242, n.33). Bryce, quoting from Thomas Mann's *Joseph and His Brethren,* also observes that "the term 'wisdom' can be morally ambiguous, 'cleverness intensified into roguishness'" (192). Nathalia Wright points to the "equivocal moral code" of the wisdom books Melville "so profusely marked in his Bible" (*Melville's Use of the Bible* [Durham: Duke University Press, 1949], 97, 94).

10. It should be observed that St. Paul's point in 1 Corinthians 13, as generally understood by several centuries of his readers, is that the structures of traditional secular wisdom are insufficient when there is no animating spirit to vivify the letter of their law and logic.

11. Sebastian Brant, "Of Blowing into Ears," in *The Ship of Fools,* trans. Edwin H. Zeydel (New York: Dover Books, 1962), 326.

12. See John Van Heijenoort, "Logical Paradoxes," in *The Encyclopedia of Philosophy,* 5:46.

13. Rosalie L. Colie, *Paradoxia Epidemica: The Renaissance Tradition of Paradox* (Princeton: Princeton University Press, 1966), 6–23, 458.

14. Browne, *Religio Medici*, 332, 396.
15. Leon Seltzer, "Camus's Absurd and the World of Melville's *The Confidence-Man*," *PMLA* 82 (1967): 21. "Logical thinking and not mere animal suffering is required for apprehension of contradictions," as Marie Collins Swabey remarks in her *Comic Laughter: A Philosophical Essay* (New Haven: Yale University Press, 1961), 11.
16. Edgar A. Dryden, *Melville's Thematics of Form: The Great Art of Telling the Truth* (Baltimore: Johns Hopkins Press, 1968), 189. Ruth A. Fox's description of *The Anatomy of Melancholy* as an exemplum of Renaissance wisdom more precisely preserves the logical paradox of Burton's (and, by analogy, Melville's) argument: "We are compelled to realize that advice is a deception of a kind, for truths are contradicted by contradictory truths, which is to say again that . . . truth is only a lie told from a different point of view" (*The Tangled Chain: The Structure of Disorder in the "Anatomy of Melancholy"* [Berkeley and Los Angeles: University of California Press, 1976], 159). If so, fictions are not simply fictitious, any more than truths are absolutely truthful. For Dryden, however, the silence that follows *The Confidence-Man* results from an unequivocal distinction between lying and truth-telling, the implication being that Melville finally broke with the logic of his own skepticism. It is on this question, dealing with the formal structure of Renaissance wisdom literature, that this essay and Dryden's study differ in emphasis. Their agreement, of course, is substantial.
17. Colie, *Paradoxia Epidemica*, 6.
18. Wright, *Melville's Use of the Bible*, 55.
19. Jane Mushabac, *Melville's Humor: A Critical Study* (Hamden, N.J.: Shoestring Press, 1981), 132. Edward H. Rosenberry describes *The Confidence-Man* as a "*perpetuum mobile*" (*Melville and the Comic Spirit* [Cambridge: Harvard University Press, 1955], 148).
20. Colie, *Paradoxia Epidemica*, 40. See H. B. de Groot, "The Ouroboros and the Romantic Poets: A Renaissance Emblem in Blake, Coleridge, and Shelley," *English Studies* (Amsterdam) 50 (1969): 553–64.
21. Dryden, *Melville's Thematics*, 191. Alan Lebowitz writes of "the deadening logic" of *The Confidence-Man* (*Progress into Silence: A Study of Melville's Heroes* [Bloomington: Indiana University Press, 1970], 187).
22. Henri Bergson, "Laughter" (1900), in *Comedy*, ed. Wylie Sypher (Garden City, N.Y.: Doubleday & Co., 1956), 80–81.
23. Reference is to Melville's letter of 2 September 1846 to John Murray, in response to the publisher's request for documentary evidence of the author's stay in the Marquesas.
24. Robert Tobias Greene's letter to the editor of the *Buffalo Commercial Adviser* (1 July 1846) testifies "to the entire accuracy of the work." Two days later, Melville wrote to Evert A. Duyckinck: "Seriously, My Dear Sir, this resurection of Toby from the dead . . . can not but settle the question of the book's genuineness" (*The Letters of Herman Melville*, ed. Merrell R. Davis and William H. Gilman [New Haven: Yale University Press, 1960], 35).
25. Henry R. Pommer, *Milton and Melville* (New York: Cooper Square, 1970), 5.
26. Nicholas Canaday Jr., *Melville and Authority* (Gainesville: University of Florida Press, 1968), 21, 11.
27. "All things work in circles"—this is the "answer of the ancients," according to Martin Farquhar Tupper's *Proverbial Philosophy* (New York: Charles Scribner, 1851), 300. Melville purchased an edition of Tupper's wisdom in September 1846.
28. Colie, *Paradoxia Epidemica*, 507. This study of paradox in the Renaissance concludes: "The paradoxist knows . . . that paradox tends toward self-contradiction

and thus toward self-destruction: only confident men can contemplate paradoxes in the first place. . ." (520).

29. David Hume, *An Enquiry concerning Human Understanding*, 12.2; cited from M. F. Burnyeat, "Can the Sceptic Live His Scepticism?" in *Doubt and Dogmatism: Studies in Hellenistic Epistemology*, ed. Malcolm Schofield, Myles Burnyeat, and Jonathan Barnes (Oxford: Clarendon Press, 1980), 24. Burnyeat answers that the skeptic cannot live his ideal of creedless rationality: "The life without belief is not an achievement of the will but a paralysis of reason by itself" (42).

30. There is hardly a Montaigne essay that does not include at least one suicide.

31. Melville, *Billy Budd and Other Prose Pieces*, 131.

32. Howard P. Vincent, *The Tailoring of Melville's "White-Jacket"* (Evanston: Northwestern University Press, 1970), 4, 108, 137, 32, 41, 36, 72.

33. Ibid., x. By this, Vincent simply means that the book is a pastiche. The suggestion here is that *White-Jacket* is a harlequin's garment, fit for hellish playing.

34. Melville, *Billy Budd and Other Prose Pieces*, 139.

35. See Charles R. Anderson, "A Reply to Herman Melville's *White-Jacket* by Rear-Admiral Thomas O. Selfridge Sr.," *American Literature* 7 (1935): 123–44.

36. The passage is from Saint-Évremond's essay, "Considération sur la religion." "We incline to think that God cannot explain His own secrets," Melville writes to Hawthorne (*Letters*, 125).

37. Saint-Évremond, "Sur la morale d'Epicure," in his *Oeuvres en prose*, ed. René Ternois (Paris: Didier, 1962–69), 3:434. Saint-Évremond wishes he were the author of Montaigne's *Essais* and *Don Quixote*.

38. References to Melville's journal are from *ML* 2:319 ff.

39. Melville records in his journal: "I told him I was" (*ML* 1:349).

40. Newton Arvin, *Herman Melville* (New York: William Sloane, 1950; reprint, Westport, Conn.: Greenwood Press, 1972), 200. See William Ellery Sedgwick, *Herman Melville: The Tragedy of Mind* (Cambridge: Harvard University Press, 1944; reprint, New York: Russell & Russell, 1962), 4–6.

41. See Eleanor Melville Metcalf, *Herman Melville: Cycle and Epicycle* (Cambridge: Harvard University Press, 1953), 108.

42. It should be observed that, unlike Melville, Montaigne clearly distinguishes between the authority of his work and that of Holy Writ. Melville here follows not Montaigne himself but his followers such as Saint-Évremond and Shaftesbury. The latter, for example, writes of St. Paul in 1 Corinthians that the apostle would not have us "depend on him as positive or certain" as to whether or not "he has the spirit"—whether "he writes by divine commission" or by "his own judgment and private opinion." The "dogmatical," as Shaftesbury reads St. Paul, is the "most dangerous state of opinion"; "the skeptical," "the safest in all likelihood" (*Characteristics of Men, Manners, Opinions, Times* [1711], ed. John M. Robertson [Indianapolis: Bobbs-Merrill, 1964], 2:203). Montaigne never argues in this way, but sharply distinguishes the folly of his own enterprise from the wisdom of sacred scripture.

43. Alfred Kazin, in his introduction to *Moby-Dick* (Boston: Houghton Mifflin Co., 1956), suggestively remarks of Ishmael's role: "he is . . . the single mind, from whose endlessly turning spool of thought the whole story is unwound" (vi).

44. See Jacob Revius, "God's Knowledge," in *European Metaphysical Poetry*, ed. Frank J. Warnke (New Haven: Yale University Press, 1961), 66–68.

45. A fiction corrects a fiction in Ronald Sutherland's novel, *Lark des Neiges* (Toronto: New Press, 1971): "At one time . . . I went right through *Moby-Dick*. . . . It's full of mistakes, I can tell you that. I checked out a few of the facts about blue whales and sperm whales and the others kinds of whales in the encyclopaedia at

school. He had them all mixed up, the author did." Another character responds that "the mistakes didn't matter a damn" (38). The mistakes did matter for Melville.

46. Rowland A. Sherrill sets this irony aside: *Moby-Dick* enacts Melville's conviction that "his prophetic speaking in fictive forms could be effectual" (*The Prophetic Melville: Experience, Transcendence and Tragedy* [Athens: University of Georgia Press, 1979], 3). For Sherrill, *Billy Budd* shows the loss of that conviction. He does not examine the much earlier *Confidence-Man*.

47. "The self-contradictory double and triple meanings of . . . words . . . produce a process of cancellation or at least a reduction which ultimately forms a restatement of the negativity of the White Whale," James William Nechas writes in *Synonymy, Repetition, and Restatement in the Vocabulary of Herman Melville's "Moby-Dick"* (Darby, Pa.: Norwood Press, 1980), 214.

48. Pearl Chester Solomon, *Dickens and Melville in Their Time* (New York: Columbia University Press, 1975), 106.

49. *"Moby-Dick" as Doubloon: Essays and Extracts, 1851–1970*, ed. Hershel Parker and Harrison Hayford (New York: W. W. Norton & Co., 1970), xix. The notion of arbitrariness as radical democracy's governing virtue is complexly promulgated in J. C. Rowe's *Through the Custom-House: Nineteenth-Century American Fiction and Modern Theory* (Baltimore: Johns Hopkins University Press, 1982). As Kenneth Dauber's review of Rowe, in *Nineteenth-Century Fiction* (38 [1983]: 243–46), reflects, "it is not clear how . . . the nihilism Rowe would forestall can, finally, be stayed." Dauber agrees with Melville.

50. John Gross remarks in his preface to *The Oxford Book of Aphorisms* (New York: Oxford University Press, 1983): "The aphorists quarrel among themselves. . . . The greatest of them tend to be haunted by irreconcilable conclusions" (viii–ix).

51. Herman Melville, "The Happy Failure," in *Billy Budd and Other Prose Pieces*, 215.

52. See John Seelye, *Melville: The Ironic Diagram* (Evanston, Ill.: Northwestern University Press, 1970), 124: Melville constructs "a full circle of metaphysical antitheses" in *The Confidence-Man*. "Elaborately interlocked insinuations, thoughout" describes Melville's syntax of opposition and inversion in *The Confidence-Man*, according to Lawrence Thompson's *Melville's Quarrel with God* (Princeton: Princeton University Press, 1952), 328.

53. Emerson, W 1:391.

54. John Bunyan, *The Pilgrim's Progress and Grace Abounding* (Boston: Houghton Mifflin Co., 1969), 89, 90, 92.

55. Ibid., 90.

56. Ibid., 155.

57. For accounts of the reader as victim in *The Confidence-Man*, see A. Carl Bredahl, Jr., *Melville's Angles of Vision* (Gainesville: University of Florida Press, 1972), 56–60; Victor-Lévy Beaulieu, *Monsieur Melville (3. l'Après 'Moby-Dick' ou la souveraine poésie)* (Montreal: VLB, 1978), 115–18; and Michael Paul Rogin, *Subversive Genealogy: The Politics and Art of Herman Melville* (New York: Knopf, 1983), 238–43.

58. See Joyce Sparer Adler, *War in Melville's Imagination* (New York: New York University Press, 1981), 111–20. The white storytellers and not the Indians are aligned with the Devil, according to Adler's revision of conventional readings of *The Confidence-Man*.

59. *Dante's Divine Comedy: The Inferno—A Literal Prose Translation*, trans. John A. Carlyle (New York: Harper & Bros., 1855), 40.

60. Carlyle, *Sartor Resartus*, 192.
61. Ibid., 193.
62. Emerson, *W* 1:135. Emerson's "aim," of course, was to speak otherwise in that address.
63. Pierre Leyris characterizes the Melvillean perspective here as "un détachement quasi asiatique" in the face of "l'engendrement réciproque et nécessaire de la vie et de la mort" (Herman Melville, *Battle Pieces, and Aspects of War*, translated and with an introduction by Pierre Leyris [Paris: Gallimard, 1981], 14).
64. *The Confidence-Man* fared much better in Britain. "A partial explanation is the failure of [British] reviewers to perceive the true depths of its disillusionments," according to Hugh W. Hetherington's *Melville's Reviewers, British and American (1846–1891)* (Chapel Hill: University of North Carolina Press, 1961), 264.
65. According to Vincent Kenny's *Herman Melville's "Clarel": A Spiritual Autobiography* (Hamden, N.J.: Shoestring Press, 1973), acceptance of man's invincible ignorance constitutes Melville's "painful wisdom" (226). See H. C. Horsford's introduction to Melville's *Journal of a Visit to Europe and the Levant* (Princeton: Princeton University Press, 1955), 18–23.
66. Compare, for example, Milton R. Stern, *The Fine Hammered Steel of Herman Melville* (Urbana: University of Illinois Press, 1968), 210; and Sedgwick, *Melville*, 249. The "double-reading of events" by *Billy Budd* commentators "leads to fantastic and unresolved involutions," the perplexed Kingsley Widmer protests in *The Ways of Nihilism: A Study of Herman Melville's Short Novels* (Los Angeles: California State Colleges, 1970), 23.
67. Melville, "Art," in *Poems*, 270.

Chapter 4. Of Blindness in Conrad's Spectacular Universe

1. Melville, *Poems*, 270.
2. Gérard Jean-Aubry, *Joseph Conrad: Life and Letters* (London: Heinemann, 1927), 2:19.
3. Joseph Conrad, *A Personal Record*, Collected Edition (London: J. M. Dent, 1946–55), 36 (all subsequent references to Conrad's works are from this edition).
4. See Gerald Morgan, "Narcissus Afloat," *Bulletin of the Humanities Association of Canada* 15 (1964): 44–55; reprinted in the Norton Critical Edition of *The Nigger of the "Narcissus,"* ed. Richard Kimbrough (1979): "the *Heart of Darkness* theme is rehearsed" in the ship *Narcissus*. The self in quest of the self wanders endlessly in circuits in this nautical tale of "communal introspection" (272–73).
5. Schopenhauer, *World as Will and Idea*, 1:346.
6. See La Bossière, *Joseph Conrad and the Science of Unknowing*, for a treatment of the *coincidentia oppositorum* in the opus as a whole.
7. Ter Horst, *Calderón*, 35–36. For an account of Conrad's references to another Calderón play, *Life Is a Dream*, see La Bossière, *Joseph Conrad*, 13, 91.
8. Matthew Arnold, *Discourses in America* (1885): "His [Emerson's] relation to us is . . . like that of the Roman Emperor Marcus Aurelius." Cited from Michael Moran, "Ralph Waldo Emerson," in *The Encyclopedia of Philosophy*, 2:479, where Arnold's comparison is offered as a commonplace summarizing Emerson's spiritual contribution to his age.
9. Edward Garnett, "Conrad's Place in English Literature," in *Conrad's Prefaces to His Works* (London: J. M. Dent, 1937; reprint, Freeport, N.J.: Books for Libraries Press, 1971), 25.
10. Edward W. Said, *Joseph Conrad and the Fiction of Autobiography* (Cam-

bridge: Harvard University Press, 1966), 137–38. This point is developed in William W. Bonney's "'Eastern Logic under my Western eyes': Conrad, Schopenhauer, and the Orient," the opening chapter of his *Thorns & Arabesques: Contexts for Conrad's Fiction* (Baltimore: Johns Hopkins University Press, 1980).

11. See, for example, Jacques Darras, *Joseph Conrad and the West: Signs of Empire* (Totowa, N.J.: Barnes & Noble, 1982), 7: Conrad's "intimate duplicity" is described as the articulation of "a fork—diabolic tongues running after their problematic unity," in linguistic structures obliterating themselves in the process of their construction.

12. Lionel Trilling, *Sincerity and Authenticity* (Cambridge: Harvard University Press, 1972), 109. "Strangely," however, should not be taken to suggest that such a movement is uncharacteristic of Conrad's fiction. As Stephen K. Land's *Paradox and Polarity in the Fiction of Joseph Conrad* (London: Macmillan; New York: St. Martin's Press, 1984) recently repeats, movement in two opposite directions at once is a "fundamental constant" in Conrad's works. Like Bonney, Land links that movement to the Schopenhauerian paradox that "purposive action is self-nullifying" (2). The strong possibility that Conrad copied from Schopenhauer's *World as Will and Idea* the lines from Calderón's *Life Is a Dream* that provided the epigraph for his second novel, *An Outcast of the Islands*, adds strength to the link. "Pues el delito mayor / Del hombre es haber nacito" (Man's greatest crime is to have been born) appears twice in Schopenhauer's monument to deconstruction (1:328, 458).

13. C. B. Cox, in his introduction to the 1974 New Dent Edition of the 1902 *Youth* volume (vii).

14. Ibid., xiv.

15. Arnold E. Davidson, *Conrad's Endings: A Study of the Five Major Novels* (Ann Arbor: UMI Research Press, 1984), 101.

16. Carlyle, *Sartor Resartus*, 79, 83.

17. Vladimir Nabokov, *Pale Fire* (1962; reprint, New York: Berkley, 1972), 166, 6.

18. R. B. Cunninghame Graham, in his preface to the 1925 Dent Edition of *Tales of Hearsay* (xiii). And yet, Cunninghame Graham imagines Conrad as a luminary, a brilliant fixed star, a light from the heavens to guide travelers in the dark desert of life (vii–viii, xv).

19. Carlyle, *Sartor Resartus*, 83–84.

20. *The Collected Letters of Joseph Conrad*, ed. F. R. Karl and Laurence Davies (Cambridge: Cambridge University Press, 1983), 1:67–68.

21. Ibid., 1:68 n.1.

22. Plutarch, "Timoléon," in *Vies*, edited and translated by Robert Flacelière and Emile Chambry (Paris: Les Belles Lettres, 1964), 4:56.

23. Ibid., 4:34: "La Fortune ... utilise un événement pour en susciter un autre, les rapproche tous de loin et entremêle ceux qui paraissent être les plus différents et n'avoir entre eux rien de commun, en les disposant de manière que la fin de l'un soit le principe de l'autre."

24. Ibid., 4:56: "ce n'est pas que la Fortune lui eût joué un mauvais tour."

25. Whalley is also likened to a tree (187). For Shaftesbury, in "The Moralists," this figure illustrates the delightful "mutual dependency of things ... the order, union, and coherence of the whole": "All things in this world are united ... as the strong and upright oak ... is fitted to the twining branches of the vine or ivy (*Characteristics*, 2:64–65). Conrad's oak-ivy image, setting Shaftesbury's optimism on its head, has a sinister burden. It recalls the picture of a serpent fastened face to face with its victim in Dante's *Inferno*, like ivy clinging tenaciously to a tree (25.58–61).

26. Leyda, *Melville Log*, 1:380–81.
27. Dante, *Inferno*, trans. Louis Biancolli (New York: Washington Square Press, 1966), 21. See Gerald Morgan, "Sea Symbol and Myth in the Works of Joseph Conrad" (diss., Université de Montréal, 1962), 92–93. "So potent it was," Walter Pater writes of the power of love in Francesca and Paolo, that "they found themselves—well! in the *Inferno*" (*Plato and Platonism*, 107).
28. *Inferno*, trans. Biancolli, 21.
29. This author's note prefaces the *Youth* volume in the Dent's Collected Edition.
30. Carlyle, *On Heroes*, 425.
31. Ibid., 459.
32. Carlyle, *Sartor Resartus*, 18.
33. *Joseph Conrad's Letters to R. B. Cunninghame Graham*, ed. C. T. Watts (Cambridge: Cambridge University Press, 1969), 118.
34. Ibid., 65.

Postscript: The Consolation of Folly

1. Aubry, *Joseph Conrad*, 1:302; cited by David Daiches, "Joseph Conrad," in *The Novel and the Modern World* (Chicago: University of Chicago Press, 1939), 58.
2. Conrad, *A Personal Record*, xv; cited by Daiches, 58.
3. Daiches, "Joseph Conrad," 60.
4. Ibid., 58.
5. See Shackleton, *Montesquieu*, 252. The omnivorous skeptic Montesquieu's painting of the bewildering array of laws and customs in *l'Esprit des lois* suggests the work of an *"Arlequin Grotius,"* as Carlyle records ("Montesquieu," in *Critical and Miscellaneous Essays* [London: Chapman & Hall, 1899], 5:84). Montesquieu's antic playing brings Carlyle to think of Montaigne; and Shackleton, of Hume.
6. Walter Pater, *Gaston de Latour* (1910), chap. 5; cited from Dédéyan, *Montaigne chez ses amis*, 1:431.
7. Montaigne, 3.3.36. Montaigne puts these words of resignation in the mouth of Socrates.
8. David Daiches, *God and the Poets: The Gifford Lectures, 1983* (Oxford: Clarendon Press, 1984), 217.
9. Ibid., 214.
10. Ibid., 222.
11. Ibid., v–vi.
12. Holloway, *Victorian Sage*, 16, 6, 290.
13. Conrad, "A Familiar Preface" to *A Personal Record*, xi.
14. Daiches, *God and the Poets*, 88.
15. Walter Pater, *The Renaissance* (London and New York: Macmillan & Co., 1893; reprint, New York: Modern Library, n.d.), 196. Original edition 1873.
16. Alexandre Micha, in the introduction to his edition of Montaigne, writes of the *Essais:* "tout revient à fuir ou à amoindrir la douleur" (12).
17. Holloway, *Victorian Sage*, 9, 16–17.
18. Ibid., 18.
19. Wilde, *Artist as Critic*, 314, 432.
20. Friedrich Nietzsche, *Ecce Homo*, trans. Anthony M. Ludovici, in *The Complete Works*, ed. Oscar Levy (New York: Russell & Russell, 1964), 17:87. While he mocks the artist as an opiate dealer, the author of *Ecce Homo* goes on to describe the most influential of his own prophetic works as the composition of just such a

trafficker: "The whole of *Zarathustra* might be classified under the rubric music" (97). Earlier in *Ecce Homo,* Nietzsche refers to Carlyle as "that great unconscious and involuntary swindler," a godless theologian (58), and likens his own deviltry to "Montaigne's mischievousness" (38). Prefigured in Montaigne's master of musical thinking, the night-loving Zarathustra embodies the "artistic Socrates" whose advent is envisioned in *The Birth of Tragedy.* Ellmann's introduction to *The Artist as Critic* recalls André Gide's and Thomas Mann's virtual identification of Nietzsche with Wilde, and compares Wilde's reshuffling of the language of ethics with Nietzsche's transvaluation (x, xxii–xxiii).

21. Stephen Crane, "The Blue Hotel," in *The Monster* (1899); cited from *The Red Badge of Courage and Selected Prose and Poetry,* edited and with an introduction by William M. Gibson (New York: Holt, Rinehart and Winston, 1968), 3d ed., 401. H. L. Mencken suggests that this tale is one that Conrad might have written: "You will find it ["The Blue Hotel"] running from end to end of Joseph Conrad" ("Various Bad Novels," *Smart Set* 40 [July 1913]: 159).

Select Bibliography

Adler, Joyce Sparer. *War In Melville's Imagination.* New York: New York University Press, 1981.

Alexander, W. H. "Johann Georg Hamann." In vol. 3 of *The Encyclopedia of Philosophy,* edited by Paul Edwards. New York and London: Collier-Macmillan, 1967.

Amiel, Henri-Frédéric. *Fragments d'un Journal intime.* 6th ed. 2 vols. Geneva: H. Georg, 1893.

Anderson, Charles R. "A Reply to Herman Melville's *White-Jacket* by Rear-Admiral Thomas O. Selfridge Sr." *American Literature* 7 (1935): 123–44.

Arvin, Newton. *Herman Melville,* New York: William Sloane, 1950. Reprint. Westport, Conn.: Greenwood Press, 1972.

Aubry, Gérard Jean–. *Joseph Conrad: Life and Letters.* 2 vols. London: Heinemann, 1927.

Baumgarten, Murray. "Parameters of Debate: A Reading of Carlyle's Annotations of Mill's *Principles of Political Economy.*" In *Carlyle: Books & Margins,* 107–29. Santa Cruz: University Library of the University of California, 1980.

Beaulieu, Victor-Lévy. *Monsieur Melville (3. l'Après "Moby-Dick" ou la souveraine poésie).* Montreal: VLB, 1978.

Béguin, Albert. *L'Ame romantique et le rêve.* Paris: José Corti, 1939.

Bergson, Henri. "Laughter." In *Comedy,* edited by Wylie Sypher. Garden City, N.Y.: Doubleday & Co., 1956.

Biser, Eugen. "Wisdom." In *Encyclopedia of Theology: The Concise "Sacramentum Mundi,"* edited by Karl Rahner. New York: Seabury Press, 1975.

Blake, William. *The Portable Blake.* Edited by Alfred Kazin. New York: Viking Press, 1968.

Bloom, Harold. *Figures of Capable Imagination.* New York: Seabury Press, 1976.

Bonney, William W. *Thorns & Arabesques: Contexts for Conrad's Fiction.* Baltimore: Johns Hopkins University Press, 1980.

Brant, Sebastian. *The Ship of Fools.* Translated by Edwin H. Zeydel. New York: Dover Books, 1962.

Bredahl, A. Carl, Jr. *Melville's Angles of Vision.* Gainesville: University of Florida Press, 1972.

Brémond, Henri. *La Poésie pure.* Paris: Grasset, 1926.

Browne, Thomas. *Religio Medici.* In *The Consolation of Philosophy,* edited by Irwin Edman. New York: Modern Library, 1943.

Bryce, Glendon A. *A Legacy of Wisdom: The Egyptian Contribution to the Wisdom of Israel.* Lewisburg: Bucknell University Press, 1979.
Bunyan, John. *The Pilgrim's Progress and Grace Abounding.* Boston: Houghton Mifflin Co., 1969.
Burgess, Anthony. *The Novel Now.* London: Faber & Faber, 1967.
Burke, Kenneth. *Language as Symbolic Action.* Berkeley: University of California Press, 1968.
———. *A Rhetoric of Motives.* Berkeley: University of California Press, 1969.
Burke, Peter. *Montaigne.* Oxford: Oxford University Press, 1981.
Burkholder, Robert E. "The Contemporary Reception of *English Traits.*" In *Emerson Centenary Essays,* edited by Joel Myerson, 156–72. Carbondale: Southern Illinois University Press, 1982.
Burkholder, Robert E., and Joel Myerson, eds. *Critical Essays on Ralph Waldo Emerson.* Boston: G. K. Hall, 1983.
Burnyeat, M. F. "Can the Sceptic Live His Scepticism?" In *Doubt and Dogmatism: Studies in Hellenistic Epistemology,* edited by Malcolm Schofield, Myles Burnyeat, and Jonathan Barnes, 20–53. Oxford: Clarendon Press, 1980.
Bush, Ronald. "T. S. Eliot: Singing the Emerson Blues." In *Emerson: Prospect & Retrospect,* edited by Joel Porte, 179–97. Cambridge: Harvard University Press, 1982.
Butor, Michel. *Essais sur les Essais.* Paris: Gallimard, 1968.
Canaday, Nicholas, Jr. *Melville and Authority.* Gainesville: University of Florida Press, 1968.
Carlyle, Thomas. *The Complete Works of Thomas Carlyle.* Edited by H. D. Traill. 30 vols. London: Chapman & Hall, 1896–99.
———. *Critical and Miscellaneous Essays.* 5 vols. London: Chapman & Hall, 1899.
———. *Sartor Resartus and On Heroes and Hero Worship.* Introduction by W. H. Hudson. London: J. M. Dent, 1908.
Charbonnel, J.-Roger. *La Pensée italienne au XVIe siècle et le courant libertin.* Paris: E. Champion, 1919. Reprint. Geneva: Slatkine, 1969.
Chase, Robert, ed. *Melville: A Collection of Critical Essays.* Englewood Cliffs: Prentice-Hall, 1962.
Church, Richard William. *The Essays of Montaigne.* London: J. W. Parker & Son, 1857.
Coleridge, Samuel Taylor. *Biographia Literaria.* Edited by John Shawcross. 2 vols. Oxford: Oxford University Press, 1907.
———. *The Collected Letters of Samuel Taylor Coleridge.* Edited by E. L. Griggs. 6 vols. Oxford: Clarendon Press, 1956–71.
———. *The Friend.* Edited by Barbara Rooke. *The Collected Works of Samuel Taylor Coleridge,* vol. 4. London: Routledge & Kegan Paul, 1969.
———. *The Notebooks of Samuel Taylor Coleridge.* Edited by Kathleen Coburn. Vol. 1. London: Routledge & Kegan Paul, 1957.
Colie, Rosalie L. *Paradoxia Epidemica: The Renaissance Tradition of Paradox.* Princeton: Princeton University Press, 1966.
Conrad, Joseph. *The Collected Edition of the Works of Joseph Conrad.* 21 vols. London: J. M. Dent, 1946–55.

———. *The Collected Letters of Joseph Conrad.* Edited by F. R. Karl and Laurence Davies. Vol. 1. Cambridge: Cambridge University Press, 1983.

———. *Joseph Conrad's Letters to R. B. Cunninghame Graham.* Edited by C. T. Watts. Cambridge: Cambridge University Press, 1969.

Cope, Jackson I. *The Theater and the Dream.* Baltimore: Johns Hopkins University Press, 1973.

Cox, C. B. "Introduction." *Youth, Heart of Darkness and The End of the Tether.* New edition. London: J. M. Dent & Sons, 1974.

Crane, Stephen. *The Red Badge of Courage and Selected Prose and Poetry.* Edited and with an introduction by William M. Gibson. 3d ed. New York: Holt, Rinehart and Winston, 1968.

Daiches, David. *God & the Poets: The Gifford Lectures, 1983.* Oxford: Oxford University Press, 1984.

———. *The Novel and the Modern World.* Chicago: University of Chicago Press, 1939.

Dalle, Réginald. "Montaigne vu par Salvador Dali." In *Montaigne et les Essais, 1580–1980,* edited by François Moreau, Robert Granderoute, and Claude Blum, 346–47. Paris and Geneva: Champion & Slatkine, 1983.

Dante, Alighieri. *Dante's Divine Comedy: The Inferno—A Literal Prose Translation.* Translated by John A. Carlyle. New York: Harper & Bros., 1855.

———. *The Inferno.* Translated by Louis Biancolli. New York: Washington Square Press, 1966.

Darras, Jacques. *Joseph Conrad and the West: Signs of Empire.* Totowa, N.J. and London: Barnes & Noble and Macmillan, 1982.

Davidson, Arnold E. *Conrad's Endings: A Study of the Five Major Novels.* Ann Arbor: UMI Research Press, 1984.

Dédéyan, Charles. *Montaigne chez ses amis anglo-saxons: Montaigne dans le romantisme anglais et ses prolongements victoriens.* 2 vols. Paris: Boivin, 1943.

de Groot, H. B. "The Ouroboros and the Romantic Poets: A Renaissance Emblem in Blake, Coleridge, and Shelley." *English Studies* (Amsterdam) 50 (1969): 553–64.

del Rio, A. *Historia de la literatura española.* 2 vols. New York: Dryden Press, 1948.

Dibble, Jerry A. *The Pythia's Drunken Song: Carlyle's "Sartor Resartus" and the Style Problem in German Idealist Philosophy.* The Hague: Martinus Nijhoff, 1978.

Ducharme, Réjean. *Les Enfantômes.* Paris: Gallimard, 1976.

Emerson, Ralph Waldo. *The Complete Works of Ralph Waldo Emerson.* Edited by Edward Waldo Emerson. 12 vols. Centenary Edition. Boston and New York: Houghton Mifflin Co., 1903–4.

———. *The Early Lectures of Ralph Waldo Emerson.* Edited by Stephen W. Whicher et al. 3 vols. Cambridge: Harvard University Press, 1959–72.

———. *The Journals and Miscellaneous Notebooks of Ralph Waldo Emerson.* Edited by William Gilman et al. 16 vols. Cambridge: Belknap Press of Harvard University, 1960– .

———. *The Letters of Ralph Waldo Emerson.* Edited by Ralph L. Rusk. 6 vols. New York: Columbia University Press, 1939.

———. *Young Emerson Speaks: Unpublished Discourses on Many Subjects.* Edited by Arthur Cushman McGiffert, Jr. Boston: Houghton Mifflin Co., 1938.

———. ed. *Parnassus.* Boston, 1874. Reprint. Freeport, N.J.: Books for Libraries Press, 1970.

Espiau de la Maestre, André. *Humanisme classique et syncrétisme mythique chez Paul Claudel.* Paris: Honoré Champion, 1977.

Fanego, Otilio Lopez. "Quelques précisions sur Montaigne et l'inquisition espagnole." In *Montaigne et les Essais, 1580–1980,* edited by François Moreau, Robert Granderoute, and Claude Blum, 368–78. Paris and Geneva: Champion & Slatkine, 1983.

Farinelli, Arturo. *La vita è un sogno.* Torino: Fratelli Bocca, 1916.

Fish, Stanley. *Self-Consuming Artifacts: The Experience of Seventeenth-Century Literature.* Berkeley: University of California Press, 1972.

Fox, Ruth A. *The Tangled Chain: The Structure of Disorder in the "Anatomy of Melancholy."* Berkeley and Los Angeles: University of California Press, 1976.

Garnett, Edward. "Conrad's Place in English Literature." In *Conrad's Prefaces to His Works,* 3–34. London: J. M. Dent, 1937. Reprint. Freeport, N.J.: Books for Libraries Press, 1971.

Gelpi, Albert. "Emerson: The Problem of Organic Form." In *Emerson: Prophecy, Metamorphosis, and Influence.* edited by David Levin, 149–70. New York: Columbia University Press, 1975.

Gide, André. "Introduction." *Les Pages immortelles de Montaigne.* Paris and New York: Editions Corrêa and Longmans Green, 1939.

Gilson, Etienne. *History of Christian Philosophy in the Middle Ages.* New York: Random House, 1955.

———. *Reason and Revelation in the Middle Ages.* New York: Charles Scribner's Sons, 1938.

Glauser, Alfred. *Montaigne paradoxal.* Paris: A. G. Nizet, 1972.

Gross, John, ed. *The Oxford Book of Aphorisms.* New York: Oxford University Press, 1983.

Hampshire, S. N. "Hume's Place in Philosophy." *David Hume: A Symposium,* edited by D. F. Pears, 1–10. London: Macmillan & Co., 1963.

Harris, Kenneth Marc. *Carlyle and Emerson: Their Long Debate.* Cambridge: Harvard University Press, 1978.

Hay, Eloise Knapp. "Impressionism Limited." In *Joseph Conrad: A Commemoration,* edited by Norman Sherry, 54–64. London: Macmillan & Co., 1976.

Hetherington, Hugh W. *Melville's Reviewers: British and American (1846–1891).* Chapel Hill: University of North Carolina Press, 1961.

Holloway, John. *The Victorian Sage: Studies in Argument.* London: Macmillan & Co., 1953.

Hopkins, Vivian C. *Spires of Form: A Study of Emerson's Aesthetic Theory.* New York: Russell & Russell, 1965.

Houghton, Walter E. *The Victorian Frame of Mind, 1830–1870.* New Haven: Yale University Press, 1957.

Hume, David. *"Dialogues concerning Natural Religion" and the Posthumous Essays, "Of the Immortality of the Soul" and "Of Suicide."* Edited and with an introduction by Richard H. Popkin. Indianapolis: Hackett Books, 1980.

Ikeler, A. Abbott. *Puritan Temper and Transcendental Faith: Carlyle's Literary Vision.* Columbus: Ohio State University Press, 1972.

James, Henry, Jr. "The Correspondence of Carlyle and Emerson." *Century Magazine* 26 (June 1883): 265–72.

Jones, Howard Mumford, ed. *Emerson on Education: Selections.* New York: Teachers' College Press of Columbia University, 1966.

Kaufmann, Walter. *From Shakespeare to Existentialism.* New York: Beacon Press, 1959. Reprint. Garden City, N.Y.: Doubleday & Co., 1960.

Kenny, Vincent. *Herman Melville's "Clarel": A Spiritual Autobiography.* Hamden, N.J.: Shoestring Press, 1973.

Ketcham, Henry. "Biographical Introduction." *Poems of R. W. Emerson and O. W. Holmes.* New York and London: Co-operative Publishing Co., 1887.

La Bossière, Camille R. *Joseph Conrad and the Science of Unknowing.* Fredericton, N.B.: York Press, 1979.

Land, Stephen K. *Paradox and Polarity in the Fiction of Joseph Conrad.* London: Macmillan; New York: St. Martin's Press, 1984.

Leary, Lewis. *Ralph Waldo Emerson: An Interpretive Essay.* Boston: Twayne, 1980.

Lebowitz, Alan. *Progress into Silence: A Study of Melville's Heroes.* Bloomington: Indiana University Press, 1970.

Le Quesne, A. L. *Carlyle.* Oxford: Oxford University Press, 1982.

Leyda, Jay. *The Melville Log: A Documentary Life of Herman Melville, 1819–1891.* 2 vols. New York: Harcourt, Brace, 1951.

Lloyd, Henry Demarest. "Emerson's Wit and Humor." *Forum* 22 (December 1896). Reprinted in *Critical Essays on Ralph Waldo Emerson,* edited by Robert E. Burkholder and Joel Myerson, 248–58. Boston: G. K. Hall, 1983.

Loving, Jerome. *Emerson, Whitman, and the American Muse.* Chapel Hill: University of North Carolina Press, 1982.

Marovitz, Sanford E. "Emerson's Shakespeare: From Scorn to Apotheosis." *Emerson Centenary Essays,* edited by Joel Myerson, 122–55. Carbondale: Southern Illinois University Press, 1982.

Melville, Herman. *Battle Pieces, and Aspects of War.* Translated and with an introduction by Pierre Leyris. Paris: Gallimard, 1981.

———. *The Confidence-Man: His Masquerade.* Ed. Hershel Parker. New York: W. W. Norton & Co., 1971.

———. *The Letters of Herman Melville.* Edited by Merrell R. Davis and William H. Gilman. New Haven: Yale University Press, 1960.

———. *Moby-Dick.* Edited and with an introduction by Alfred Kazin. Boston: Houghton Mifflin Co., 1956.

———. *The Works of Herman Melville.* 16 vols. New York: Russell & Russell, 1963.

Mencken, H. L. "Various Bad Novels." *Smart Set* 40 (July 1930): 159.

Metcalf, Eleanor Melville. *Herman Melville: Cycle and Epicycle.* Cambridge: Harvard University Press, 1953.

Miles, Josephine. *Ralph Waldo Emerson.* Minneapolis: University of Minnesota Press, 1964.

Montaigne, Michel de. *Essais.* Edited and with an introduction by Alexandre Micha. 3 vols. Paris: Garnier-Flammarion, 1969.

———. *Essays of Michel de Montaigne.* Translated by Charles Cotton, and selected and illustrated by Salvador Dali. Garden City, N.Y.: Doubleday & Co., 1947.

Morgan, Gerald. "Harlequin Faustus: Marlowe's Comedy of Hell." *Humanities Association Bulletin* (Canada) 18 (1967):22–34.

———. "Narcissus Afloat." *Bulletin de l'Association canadienne des humanités* 15

(1964): 44–55. Reprinted in *The Nigger of the "Narcissus,"* edited by Richard Kimbrough, 262–75. New York: W. W. Norton & Co., 1979.

———. "Sea Symbol and Myth in the Works of Joseph Conrad." Diss., Université de Montréal, 1962.

Mushabac, Jane. *Melville's Humor: A Critical Study.* Hamden, N.J.: Shoestring Press, 1981.

Nabokov, Vladimir. *Pale Fire.* New York: Berkley, 1972.

Nechas, James William. *Synonymy, Repetition, and Restatement in the Vocabulary of Herman Melville's "Moby-Dick."* Darby, Pa.: Norwood Press, 1980.

Nemerov, Howard. *The Collected Poems of Howard Nemerov.* Chicago: University of Chicago Press, 1977.

———. *Journal of the Fictive Life.* Chicago: University of Chicago Press, 1965.

Neufeldt, Leonard. *The House of Emerson.* Lincoln: University of Nebraska Press, 1982.

Nicholas of Cusa. *Of Learned Ignorance.* Translated by G. Heron. 2 vols. London: Routledge & Kegan Paul, 1954.

Neitzsche, Friedrich. *Ecce Homo.* Edited by Oscar Levy. New York: Russell & Russell, 1964.

———. *Thus Spoke Zarathustra.* Translated by R. J. Hollingdale. Harmondsworth: Penguin, 1961.

Packer, B. L. *Emerson's Fall: A New Interpretation of the Major Essays.* New York: Continuum, 1982.

Parker, Alexander. *The Allegorical Drama of Calderón.* Oxford: Dolphin Press, 1968.

Parker, Hershel, and Harrison Hayford, eds. *"Moby-Dick" as Doubloon: Essays and Extracts, 1851–1970.* New York: W. W. Norton & Co., 1970.

Pascal, Blaise. *Pensées.* Edited and with an introduction by Léon Brunschigg. Paris: Le Livre de Poche, 1972.

Pater, Walter. *Plato and Platonism.* London and New York: Macmillan & Co., 1893.

———. *The Renaissance.* New York: Modern Library, n.d.

Paul, Sherman. *Emerson's Angles of Vision.* Cambridge: Harvard University Press, 1952.

Plotinus. *The Essential Plotinus: Representative Treatises from the "Enneads."* Translated and with an introduction by Elmer O'Brien. New York: New American Library, 1964.

Plutarch. *Vies.* Translated by Robert Flacelière and Emile Chambry. 16 vols. Paris: Les Belles Lettres, 1964.

Pommer, Henry R. *Milton and Melville.* New York: Cooper Square, 1970.

Porte, Joel. *Representative Man: Ralph Waldo Emerson in His Time.* New York: Oxford University Press, 1979.

Pullin, Faith, ed. *New Perspectives on Melville.* Kent, Ohio, and Edinburgh: Kent State University Press and Edinburgh University Press, 1978.

Quirk, Tom. *Melville's Confidence Man: From Knave to Knight.* Columbia: University of Missouri Press, 1982.

Revius, Jacob. "God's Knowledge." In *European Metaphysical Poetry,* edited by Frank J. Warnke, 66–68. New Haven: Yale University Press, 1961.

Richardson, Dorothy M. *Pilgrimage (IV).* London: Virago, 1979.

Rogin, Michael Paul. *Subversive Genealogy: The Politics and Art of Herman Melville.* New York: Knopf, 1983.

Rosen, Stanley. *Nihilism: A Philosophical Essay.* New Haven: Yale University Press, 1969.

Rosenberry, Edward H. *Melville and the Comic Spirit.* Cambridge: Harvard University Press, 1955.

Rousset, Jean. *Circé et le paon: La littérature de l'âge baroque en France.* Paris: José Corti, 1954.

Rowe, J. C. *Through the Custom-House: Nineteenth-Century American Fiction and Modern Theory.* Baltimore: Johns Hopkins University Press, 1982.

Rusk, Ralph L. *The Life of Ralph Waldo Emerson.* New York: Columbia University Press, 1949.

Said, Edward. *Joseph Conrad and the Fiction of Autobiography.* Cambridge: Harvard University Press, 1966.

Sainte-Beuve, Charles-Augustin. *Port-Royal.* Edited by René Louis Doyon and Charles Marchesné. Vol. 3. Paris: La Connaissance, 1926.

Saint-Évremond, Charles de. *Oeuvres en prose.* Edited by René Ternois. 4 vols. Paris: Didier, 1962–69.

Santayana, George. "Ralph Waldo Emerson." In *American Prose: Selections with Critical Introductions by Various Writers,* edited by George Rice Carpenter. New York: Macmillan, 1898. Reprinted in *Critical Essays on Ralph Waldo Emerson,* edited by Robert E. Burkholder and Joel Myerson, 258–63. Boston: G. K. Hall, 1983.

Schopenhauer, Arthur. *The World as Will and Idea.* Translated by R. B. Haldane. 3 vols. London: Routledge & Kegan Paul, 1883–86.

Sealts, Merton M., Jr. "Emerson as Teacher." In *Emerson Centenary Essays,* edited by Joel Myerson, 180–90. Carbondale: Southern Illinois University Press, 1982.

Sedgwick, William Ellery. *Herman Melville: The Tragedy of Mind.* Cambridge: Harvard University Press, 1944. Reprint. New York: Russell & Russell, 1962.

Seelye, John. *Melville: The Ironic Diagram.* Evanston: Northwestern University Press, 1970.

Seward, Barbara. *The Symbolic Rose.* New York: Columbia University Press, 1960.

Shackleton, Robert. *Montesquieu: A Critical Biography.* Oxford: Oxford University Press, 1961.

Shaftesbury, Anthony Ashley Cooper, Third Earl of. *Characteristics of Men, Manners, Opinions, Times.* Edited by John M. Robertson. 2 vols. in one. Indianapolis: Bobbs-Merrill Co., 1964.

Sherrill, Rowland A. *The Prophetic Melville: Experience, Transcendence and Tragedy.* Athens: University of Georgia Press, 1979.

Slater, John, ed. *The Correspondence of Emerson and Carlyle.* New York: Columbia University Press, 1964.

Smith, Gayle L. "Reading Emerson on the Right Side of the Brain." *Modern Language Studies* 15 (1985): 24–31.

Solomon, Pearl Chester. *Dickens and Melville.* New York: Columbia University Press, 1975.

Sterling, John. *Essays & Tales.* Edited by Julius Charles Hare. 2 vols. London: W. H. Parker, 1848.

———. "Montaigne and His Writings." *London and Westminster Review* 29 (August 1838): 321–52.
Stern, Milton R. *The Fine Hammered Steel of Herman Melville*. Urbana: University of Illinois Press, 1968.
Sukenick, Ronald. "Art from the Underground." *American Book Review* 6 (January–February 1984): 2–3.
Sullivan, Henry. *Calderón in the German lands and the Low Countries: His Reception and Influence, 1654–1980*. Cambridge: Cambridge University Press, 1983.
Sutherland, Ronald. *Lark des Neiges*. Toronto: New Press, 1971.
Swabey, Marie Collins. *Comic Laughter: A Philosophical Essay*. New Haven: Yale University Press, 1961.
Sypher, Wylie. *Four Stages of Renaissance Style*. New York: Doubleday & Co., 1955.
Ter Horst, Robert. *Calderón: The Secular Plays*. Lexington: University of Kentucky Press, 1982.
Thompson, Lawrence. *Melville's Quarrel with God*. Princeton: Princeton University Press, 1952.
Trilling, Lionel. *Sincerity and Authenticity*. Cambridge: Harvard University Press, 1972.
Vansteenberghe, Edmond. *Le Cardinal Nicholas de Cues*. Paris: Minerve, 1920.
Vincent, Howard P. *The Tailoring of Melville's "White-Jacket."* Evanston: Northwestern University Press, 1970.
von Rad, Gerhard. *Wisdom in Israel*. Translated by James D. Martin. London: SCM, 1972.
Watt, Ian. *Conrad in the Nineteenth Century*. Berkeley: University of California Press, 1979.
Widmer, Kingsley. *The Ways of Nihilism: A Study of Herman Melville's Short Novels*. Los Angeles: California State Colleges, 1970.
Wilde, Oscar. *The Artist as Critic*. Edited by Richard Ellmann. New York: Random House 1969. Reprint, Chicago: University of Chicago Press, 1982.
Wilhelm, Kate. *The Infinity Box*. New York: Harper & Row, 1977.
Wright, Nathalia. *Melville's Use of the Bible*. Durham: Duke University Press, 1949.

Index

Adler, George J., 70
Adler, Joyce Sparer, 115 n.58
Alcott, Amos Bronson, 39, 109 n.21
Almanack of the Month, 63
Amiel, Henri-Frédéric, 34
Anatomy of Melancholy, 62, 113 n.16
Anaxagoras, 25
Aristotle, 53, 61, 65
Arnold, Matthew, 89
Arvin, Newton, 71

Baumgarten, Murray, 107 n.85
Beaulieu, Victor-Lévy, 115 n.57
Bergson, Henri, 62
Berkeley, Bishop George, 46, 65
Biathanatos, 66
Biser, Eugen, 9
Blackwood's Magazine, 64, 65, 68
Blake, William, 44, 47
Bloom, Harold, 15, 16
Bon Homme Richard, 78
Bonney, William W., 117 nn. 10 and 12
Brant, Sebastian, 61
Bredahl, A. Carl, Jr., 115 n.57
Brémond, Abbé Henri, 25
Browne, Sir Thomas, 60, 61, 65, 66
Bryce, Glendon A., 112 n.9
Bunyan, John, 81–83
Burgess, Anthony, 106 n.16
Burke, Kenneth, 32–33, 106 n.69
Burkholder, Robert E., 54
Burnyeat, M. F., 114 n.29
Butor, Michel, 30

Calderón de la Barca, Pedro, 25–28, 88, 105 nn. 28 and 31, 117 n.12
Calvert, George Henry, 110 n.38
Canaday, Nicholas, Jr., 65
Carlyle, Dr. John, 47, 83

Carlyle, Thomas, 9, 10, 15–19, 20–37, 65, 66, 84; and Conrad, 17–18, 30, 90; and Emerson, 21–22, 28–29, 30, 33, 37, 38–41, 42, 57, 108 n.12; and Montaigne, 20–37, 118 n.5. Works: *French Revolution*, 40; *On Heroes*, 17, 28–29, 97; *Sartor Resartus*, 28–36, 39, 97
Channing, William Ellery, 109 n.21
Chase, Richard, 59
Church, Richard William, 18
Cicero, Marcus Tullius, 56
Claudel, Paul, 36
Clough, Arthur Hugh, 38–39
Coleridge, Samuel Taylor, 22, 28, 58, 110 n.48, 111 n.51
Colie, Rosalie L., 61, 62, 66
Conrad, Joseph, 9, 10, 16–18, 38, 86–101; and Carlyle, 17–18, 30, 35, 36, 90; and Crane, 119 n.20; and Dante, 33; and Emerson, 89, 90; and Melville, 86–87, 88, 89, 96; and Montaigne, 10, 18, 88, 89, 90–91, 94, 96, 97, 99. Works: *End of the Tether*, 92–97; *Heart of Darkness*, 18, 87, 89–90, 93, 101; *Notes on Life and Letters*, 88–90; *Personal Record*, 17–19, 98, 100; Preface to *The Nigger of the "Narcissus,"* 17–18, 100; *Victory*, 88, 98–99
Cope, Jackson I., 27
Cox, C. B., 90
Cranch, Charles Pearse, 108 n.12
Crane, Stephen, 101, 119 n.20
Cunninghame Graham, R. B., 91, 117 n.18
Cusa, Cardinal Nicholas of, 27–28, 61

Daiches, David, 98–101
Daily Knickerbocker, 64
Dali, Salvador, 46

Dante Alighieri, 28, 32–33, 47–48, 50, 56, 65, 78, 80, 83, 96, 99, 117 n.25
Darras, Jacques, 117 n.11
Dauber, Kenneth, 115 n.49
Davidson, Arnold E., 90
Dédéyan, Charles, 15, 21–22, 27
De finibus, 56
De Quincey, Thomas, 70
Dibble, Jerry A., 31
Doherty, Joseph F., 52
Donne, John, 66
Dryden, Edgar A., 62, 113 n.16
Ducharme, Réjean, 24
Duyckinck, Evert A., 71, 113 n.24

Ecclesiastes, Book of, 44, 61–62, 65–66, 69, 73, 75–76, 77, 85
Edinburgh Encyclopaedia, 21
Emerson, Ralph Waldo, 9, 10, 18, 28–29, 38–58, 84; and Carlyle, 21–22, 28–29, 30, 33, 37, 38–41, 42, 108 n.12; and Conrad, 89, 90; and Dante, 47–48; and Melville, 40, 42, 84; and Milton, 43–44, 47–48; and Montaigne, 21, 24, 28–29, 31–32, 37, 39, 41, 43–48, 51–53, 56, 57, 109 n.21
Erasmus, Desiderius, 61, 65
Espiau de la Maestre, André, 36
Eubulides of Miletus, 61

Fish, Stanley, 10, 104 n.23
FitzGerald, Edward, 105 n.28
Flying Dutchman, 58
Fox, George, 24
Fox, Ruth A., 113 n.16
Franklin, Benjamin, 78
Fraser's Magazine, 29

Garnett, Edward, 88
Gide, André, 24, 47, 119 n.20
Gifford, Mrs. Ellen Marett, 59
Glauser, Alfred, 24, 25, 30
Godey's Lady's Book, 76
Goethe, Johann Wolfgang von, 28, 34, 36, 42, 107 n.85
Greene, Richard Tobias, 63, 113 n.24

Hamann, Johann Georg, 27
Harlequin, figure of, 9, 33, 44, 60, 69, 70, 90, 114 n.33
Harris, Kenneth Marc, 20, 21, 36, 39
Hawthorne, Nathaniel, 62, 68, 96

Hay, Eloise Knapp, 18
Hazlitt, William, 84–85
Hedge, F. H., 109 n.21
Heller, Joseph, 98
Heraclitus, 41, 46, 109 n.21
Herbert, George, 76, 99
Hetherington, Hugh W., 117 n.64
Hoffmann, E. T. A., 28
Holloway, John, 10, 15–19, 100–101
Home Journal, 63
Hopkins, Vivian C., 108 n.12
Houghton, Walter E., 15
Hudson, W. H., 33
Hume, David, 15–16, 18, 27–28, 33, 35, 46, 66, 99, 105 n.31, 114 n.29, 118 n.5

Ibsen, Henrik, 9
Ikkeler, A. Abbott, 20, 33

James, Henry, Jr., 20
Jones, Howard Mumford, 108 n.12
Jones, John Paul, 78
Journal des débats, 63
Joyce, James, 9

Kant, Immanuel, 27, 105 n.40
Kaufmann, Walter, 10
Kazin, Alfred, 72
Kenny, Vincent P., 116 n.65
Ketcham, Henry, 40

La Bossière, Camille R., 116 n.6
Land, Stephen K., 117 n.12
Lanier, Sidney, 41
Leary, Lewis, 50
Lebowitz, Alan, 113 n.21
Le Quesne, A. L., 9, 107–8 n.6
Lesage, Alain-René, 92
Levin, David, 42
Leyris, Pierre, 116 n.63
Life and Remarkable Adventures of Israel R. Potter, 77
Life of Timoleon, 92–93
Lloyd, Henry Demarest, 41
London and Westminster Review, 20
Loving, Jerome, 111 n.57
Lowell, James Russell, 41
Luther, Martin, 23, 24, 36, 80

Mann, Thomas, 119 n.20
Marcus Aurelius, 89
Marlowe, Christopher, 44, 110 n.39

Index

Marovitz, Sanford E., 54
Melville, Herman, 9, 10, 18, 59–85; and Carlyle, 65, 66, 84; and Conrad, 86–87, 88, 89; and Emerson, 40, 42, 84; and Montaigne, 59–60, 65–67, 70, 73, 74–75, 84, 114 n.42. Works: "Art," 60, 85, 86; *The Confidence-Man,* 59–62, 79–85; "Conflict of Convictions," 83; *Israel Potter,* 77–79; *Mardi,* 65–67, 74, 76; *Moby-Dick,* 72–74; *Omoo,* 64–65; *Pierre,* 74–76; *Redburn,* 67–68; *Typee,* 63–64; *White-Jacket,* 67–70
Mencken, H. L., 119 n.20
Miles, Josephine, 108 n.12
Milton, John, 40, 43–44, 57, 99, 110 n.48
"Moby-Dick" as Doubloon, 74
Montaigne, Michel de, 9, 10, 15–19, 20–37, 38, 41, 43–48, 51–53, 56, 57, 59–60, 65–67, 69, 70, 73–75, 86, 87, 88, 89–91, 94, 99, 101, 109 n.21, 114 n.42, 118 n.5, 118–19 n.20
Moon Queen and King Knight: or Harlequin Twilight, 70
Morgan, Gerald, 44, 110 n.39, 116 n.4, 118 n.27
Mushabac, Jane, 62

Nabokov, Vladimir, 90
Nechas, James William, 115 n.47
Nemerov, Howard, 49, 111 n.54
Newcomb, Charles, 109 n.21
New York Press, 85
Nietzsche, Friedrich Wilhelm, 49, 101, 111 n.53, 118–19 n.20
Novalis, 17, 30

O'Brien, Elmer, 109 n.21
O'Neill, John, 24
Opposites, balance of, 9, 19, 24, 28–29, 31, 35, 36, 64, 101; coincidence of, 9, 10, 22–23, 25, 27, 33, 49–50, 54, 60, 69, 80, 85, 87, 110 n.48, 111 n.50
Ouroboros, 30, 48, 50, 62, 66, 73, 90, 111 n.51, 113 n.20
Ovid, 32, 48

Pascal, Blaise, 24, 35
Pater, Walter, 15–16, 99, 100–101, 118 n.27
Paul, Saint (the apostle), 61, 65–66, 71, 79–80, 82–83, 112 n.9, 114 n.42

Peabody, Elizabeth Palmer, 50
Philaster, 70
Philosophy for the People, 42
Pilgrim's Progress, 81–83
Plato, 15, 18, 51–52, 53
Plotinus, 41, 109 n.21
Plutarch, 41, 92–93
Pommer, Henry R., 65
Poor Richard's Almanack, 78
Poradowska, Marguerite, 91–92
Porphyry, 76
Porte, Joel, 50, 110 n.39
Protagoras, 19
Pullin, Faith, 59
Putnam's Monthly Magazine, 79

Quirk, Thomas, 59

Rabelais, François, 65, 80
Renaissance, 100
Revius, Jacob, 72
Richardson, Dorothy, 40
Rime of the Ancient Mariner, 58
Rogin, Michael Paul, 115 n.57
Rosen, Stanley, 51
Rosenberry, Edward H., 113 n.19
Rosencrantz, J. K. F., 28
Rousseau, Jean-Jacques, 9
Rousset, Jean, 10, 46
Rowe, J. C., 115 n.49
Rusk, Ralph L., 20, 22

Said, Edward W., 89
Santayana, George, 50
Saint-Evremond, Charles de, 16, 69, 114 n.42
Sainte-Beuve, Charles-Augustin, 16, 23
Schopenhauer, Arthur, 26–27, 33, 85, 88, 104 n.40, 117 n.12
Schuyler, Montgomery, 98
Sedgwick, W. E., 116 n.66
Seelye, John, 79
Selfridge, Admiral Thomas O., Sr., 69
Seltzer, Leon, 62
Seward, Barbara, 32
Sextus Empiricus, 24
Shaftesbury, third earl of, 114 n.42, 117 n.25
Shakespeare, William, 16, 26, 27, 28, 34, 54, 65, 67, 68
Shaw, Elizabeth K., 64
Ship of Fools, 61

Sirach, Book of, 44, 60–61
Slater, Joseph, 20, 41
Socrates, 15, 16, 18–19, 45
Solomon, Pearl Chester, 74
Sterling, John, 11, 20, 36, 38–39, 40
Stern, Milton R., 116 n.66
Sterne, Lawrence, 70
Stewart, Dugald, 35
Sukenick, Ronald, 109 n.31
Sullivan, Henry, 28
Sutherland, Ronald, 114–15 n.45
Swabey, Mary Collins, 113 n.15
Sypher, Wylie, 27

Ter Horst, Robert, 26, 88, 106 n.49
Thomas Aquinas, Saint, 23

Thompson, Lawrence, 115 n.52
Thoreau, Henry David, 109 n.21
Trilling, Lionel, 90
Tristram Shandy, 70
Tupper, Martin Farquhar, 113 n.27

Vincent, Howard P., 69
von Rad, Gerhard, 60

Wandering Jew, 58
Webster, Daniel, 109 n.21
Werner, Zacharias, 107 n.85
Widmer, Kingsley, 116 n.66
Wilde, Oscar, 34, 40, 98, 101, 119 n.20
Wilhelm, Kate, 24
Wright, Nathalia, 62, 112 n.9